P9-BBP-650

# TRAIN SMART

## Second Edition

*For Duke . . .*
*Friendship at its best*

# TRAIN SMART

**Effective
Trainings
Every Time**

Rich Allen

Second Edition

**CORWIN PRESS**
A SAGE Publications Company
Thousand Oaks, CA 91320

Copyright © 2008 by Corwin Press

All rights reserved. When forms and sample documents are included, their use is authorized only by educators, local school sites, and/or noncommercial and nonprofit entities who have purchased the book. Except for that usage, no part of this book may be reproduced or utilized in any form or by any means, electronic or mechanical, including photocopying, recording, or by any information storage and retrieval system, without permission in writing from the publisher.

*For information:*

Corwin Press
A Sage Publications Company
2455 Teller Road
Thousand Oaks, California 91320
www.corwinpress.com

Sage Publications India Pvt. Ltd.
B 1/I 1 Mohan Cooperative
Industrial Area
Mathura Road, New Delhi 110 044
India

Sage Publications Ltd.
1 Oliver's Yard
55 City Road
London EC1Y 1SP
United Kingdom

Sage Publications Asia-Pacific Pte. Ltd.
33 Pekin Street #02-01
Far East Square
Singapore 048763

Printed in the United States of America

**Library of Congress Cataloging-in-Publication Data**

Allen, Rich (Richard)
TrainSmart: Effective trainings every time/Rich Allen.—2nd ed.
     p. cm.
Previously published: San Diego, CA: Brain Store, c2001.
Includes bibliographical references and index.
ISBN 978-1-4129-5577-5 (cloth: alk. paper)
ISBN 978-1-4129-5578-2 (pbk.: alk. paper)
     1. Employees—Training of. 2. Training. 3. Employee training personnel.
I. Title. II. Title: Train smart.

HF5549.5.T7A469 2008
658.3'124—dc22

2007007913

This book is printed on acid-free paper.

07   08   09   10   11   12   10   9   8   7   6   5   4   3   2   1

| | |
|---|---|
| *Acquisitions Editor:* | Cathy Hernandez |
| *Editorial Assistant:* | Megan Bedell |
| *Production Editors:* | Denise Santoyo and Jenn Reese |
| *Copy Editor:* | Susan Jarvis |
| *Typesetter:* | C&M Digitals (P) Ltd. |
| *Indexer:* | Judy Hunt |
| *Cover Designer:* | Lisa Miller |

Cartoons on pages 8, 10, 14, 17, 25, 47, 66, 96, 115, 127, and 133 © Education Illustrated, LLC. Used by permission.

# Contents

# Preface to the Second Edition

Organizational training has moved on a quite a bit since I first wrote *TrainSmart* in 2001. I was startled to discover the original version featured pictures of overhead projectors and the music section had no mention of MP3s!

But it's not just technology that has changed our lives as trainers. As organizations have pared costs to the bone, the spotlight of "value for money" is well and truly shining on the training dollar. Just think about how evaluations have changed in the last few years. Remember the days of "did you like the facilitator's jokes?" check-box sheets at the end of the program? Now we have sophisticated, embedded evaluation processes to check whether participants actually learned anything and whether their productivity has improved as a result.

So I figured it was time to revise *TrainSmart*, both to help trainers rise to the challenges of this new, performance-focused environment and to reflect the new technologies now at our disposal.

If you're a previous reader, in addition to discussions of new technologies and my latest training strategies, you'll find more examples and tips, and a matrix that pulls the concepts together. I also hope you like the new images that support the concepts. I included them because if we're not having fun, we're not learning—right?

To new readers: welcome! You're about to join a worldwide community of TrainSmart facilitators. People who train smarter, not harder. People who create dynamic learning experiences and produce amazing results.

TrainSmart is about making you a more effective trainer. But it's also about making training more enjoyable for YOU. I hope it renews your enthusiasm for learning and teaching.

Once you've tried out a few of the strategies, feel free to e-mail me at rich@educationillustrated.com and let me know how your workshops are going!

# Acknowledgments

Over the past twenty-five years, I have had the opportunity to work with a number of extraordinarily gifted individuals. I am grateful that each of them has been such an important part of my professional life.

Susan Adams

Tim Andrews

Scott Bornstein

Laura Bowen

Linda Brown

Phil Bryson

Craig Bulmer

Dr. Stephanie Burns

Peter Coldicott

Bobbi DePorter

David Edwards

Dr. Billie Enz

Dr. Donald J. Freeman

Judy Green

Sean Hall

Michael Hann

Allison Helstrup

Jan Hensley

Eric Jensen

Rob Jensen

Duke Kelly

Kellie King

Pete LaGrego

John LeTellier

Dee Lindenberger

Dr. James McCray

Doug McBride

Dr. Cristal McGill

Jim Moore

Kate Neal

Bill Payne

Mark Reardon

Tiffany Reindl

Timothy Giles Rickett

Richard Scheaff

Sarah Singer-Nourie

Lance Tomlinson

Nic Veltman

Laura Wilde

Larry Wilson

Two people have greatly contributed to the process of updating this book, and deserve special thanks: Dr. Cristal McGill for reviewing and updating the research, and Karen Pryor for helping me alter the book's tone so it more accurately models the strategies. Finally, thanks to my new St. Croix family: Alonzo, Deb, Judi and Scott, Val and Denny, Ted and Sam, Jed, Henry, Lori, Paulie G., and the entire staff of Duggans—class acts all of you!

## Publisher's Acknowledgments

Corwin Press gratefully acknowledges the contributions of the following reviewers:

Curtis A. Cain, Director of Curriculum &
    Professional Development
Park Hill School District, Kansas City, MO

Mollie S. Guion, Professional Development Specialist
Austin Independent School District, Austin, TX

Mary Ann Hartwick, Instructional Coach
Litchfield Elementary School District, Litchfield, AZ

Betty Roqueni, Principal
William V. Wright Elementary, Las Vegas, NV

Nancy Skerritt, Assistant Superintendent
Tahoma School District, Maple Valley, WA

Robert Sylwester, Emeritus Professor of Education
University of Oregon, Eugene, OR

# About the Author

 **Rich Allen** is an international consultant with more than twenty-five years' experience coaching trainers and educators. Cofounder and President of Education Illustrated, he has taken the TrainSmart strategies beyond the United States and Canada to such diverse countries as the United Kingdom, Australia, New Zealand, Hong Kong, Singapore, Brunei, Russia, Jordan, and Brazil. Allen is also a popular keynote speaker at international conferences and facilitates motivational and teambuilding workshops for the top management of such prominent organizations as PriceWaterhouseCoopers, L'Oreal, IBM, the New Zealand Defense Force, Action International, General Motors, KiwiBank, Dupont, and Porsche.

Dr. Allen first took to the stage as an off-Broadway actor before starting his educational career as a high-school math and drama teacher. In 1985 he became a lead facilitator for SuperCamp—an accelerated learning program for teens—and has since worked with more than 25,000 students worldwide. He completed his doctorate in educational psychology at Arizona State University, where he studied how the human brain receives, processes, and recalls information—knowledge that informs all aspects of his training strategies.

The author resides in the U.S. Virgin Islands on the sun-kissed paradise of St. Croix, and can be reached at his e-mail address: rich@educationillustrated.com.

*"If the bum is numb, the brain's the same."*

# PART ONE

# Prepare for Effective Trainings Every Time

**Overview**

**The Five Pillars of the TrainSmart Model**

1. Engage—Prepare the Mind for Learning
2. Frame—Establish the Relevance of the Learning Material
3. Explore—Involve and Engage Participants in the Material
4. Debrief—Consolidate the Learning
5. Reflect—Embed the Learning

**The Bricks and Mortar of the TrainSmart Model**

The Bricks . . .

1. *Teach People, Not Content*
2. *Awareness Leads to Choice*
3. *Learning + Enjoyment = Retention*
4. *Application Is Everything*
5. *Stories Work*

*(Continued)*

(Continued)

> . . . and Mortar
>    *1. Crest of the Wave*
>    *2. Frames Create Meaning*
>    *3. Make It Memorable*
>    *4. Open Loops*
>    *5. Train Directly to the Point*
> **A Sample TrainSmart Schedule**

# Overview

Although *TrainSmart* covers a great deal of territory, you'll find you can internalize the principles and strategies swiftly because they're inherent to how the brain naturally learns best. Therefore, they should make *perfect sense* to you. And, perhaps most important, they will give your participants a better chance of learning and even allow them to enjoy the experience.

As you begin journeying into TrainSmart territory, you'll probably start thinking about how to apply the strategies to your own training, so the book includes spaces for you to jot down your ideas as you go.

*Part One* introduces you to the TrainSmart approach—the pillars and foundation upon which the model is built.

*Part Two* outlines the twenty-five Key Concepts that transform the model into practical applications you can implement immediately.

*Part Three* presents a handful of powerful parables that will linger in the minds of your learners long after your closing remarks. It also concludes with a checklist and a lesson plan template to help you build the TrainSmart strategies into your own training.

The TrainSmart strategies are based on my twenty-five years of experience as a trainer and educator; they have been tested and proven by teachers and trainers all over the world. Together, they form a model that reflects the art and science of *training smarter, not harder.* Let's take a closer look.

# The Five Pillars of the TrainSmart Model

TrainSmart uses the term *model* to mean "a preliminary construction that serves as a plan from which a final product is made," so you need

**Figure 1.1** The Five Pillars of the TrainSmart Model

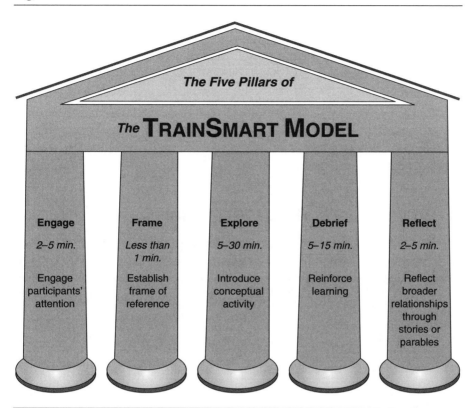

to customize it to meet the requirements of your particular training situation. In other words, the TrainSmart model gives you only a basic framework: it requires *your* creativity, planning, and purposeful action to make it work.

The five pillars in Figure 1.1 represent the action steps of the TrainSmart model. Ideally, you should include them in every training plan. Of course, *how* and *when* you incorporate them will depend on your own personal style, objectives, environment, and experience.

## 1. Engage—Prepare the Mind for Learning

This step doubles as an *energizer* and/or an *icebreaker* if needed. However, its primary purpose is to mentally prepare participants for the learning session ahead. In this step, we bring participants into the moment, screen out distractions, remove the anxiety of being in an unfamiliar setting, and focus their brains.

## 2. Frame—Establish the Relevance of the Learning Material

This step allows us both to address participants' concerns, so they can concentrate on learning, and explain the immediate learning objective(s). It should answer such questions as:

- Why am I here?
- What am I supposed to learn?
- How is this information important to me?
- How will this new knowledge benefit me either personally or professionally?

## 3. Explore—Involve and Engage Participants in the Material

This active step introduces participants to the key content of our training—not by telling them about it, but by involving them in it. Good exploration activities involve sensory experiences and attention to a variety of learning styles and multiple intelligences. This type of active exploration is vital because when we stimulate participants on multiple levels—physically, mentally, socially, and/or emotionally—we improve their comprehension and recall.

## 4. Debrief—Consolidate the Learning

This step highlights and reinforces the key points of our training. It typically involves facilitating participant dialogue and/or interaction relating to the prior exploration activity. This step also helps us to determine what content participants have internalized and where we need to elaborate further. The key in this stage is to *guide* participants toward a clear understanding of the content.

## 5. Reflect—Embed the Learning

The reflection step often incorporates a parable, personal example, or metaphor to illustrate the concept in a real-life context. It's where we help participants identify the broader meaning of the content. Ideally, it should leave learners with a deep and lasting impression of the material.

The real-life example on the following page illustrates what the TrainSmart model might look like when incorporated into a sales seminar for realtors.

## A Real-Life Training Example

**What:**
A sales seminar for realtors

**Purpose:**
Train new realtors in the art of building relationships with customers

**Action Steps:**

**Engage**

Ask participants to pair up and simulate a situation in which they're meeting each other for the first time. Have the pairs decide which of them will play the part of the realtor and which the client. Either meet with the realtors briefly or pass a card to each of them explaining their specific role—that of a very rude salesperson. When the role play gets under way, the client is baffled as she or he attempts to make a positive contact. This unexpected exercise gets everyone laughing and helps to release the anxiety inherent in a new learning environment.

**Frame**

Use a PowerPoint slide or flip-chart diagram to illustrate "The Anatomy of a Real Estate Sale." The diagram reflects the areas of content that will be covered in the training. Explain the value of the skill they are about to learn and how it will be of benefit to them.

**Explore**

After a brief explanation of the brainstorming process, divide the audience into small groups to brainstorm the essential elements of a successful first contact between a realtor and potential client. Ask a volunteer in each group to record the ideas generated by the group. Afterward, have the groups share their responses with the entire class. Then ask for volunteer pairs to demonstrate a refined first contact for the class, this time incorporating as many positive elements as possible.

*(Continued)*

(Continued)

**Debrief**

As a follow-up to the exploration activity, ask the seated participants to evaluate the scene they've just observed. Provide guiding questions such as, (1) What worked? (2) What didn't work? (3) Would you have done anything differently? (4) Would you have been impressed if you were the client? Then pose broader questions such as, (5) Is there a single *correct* way to greet a new client? (6) What might you want to consider when sizing up the client and steering the interaction? Rather than *telling* them, *guide* participants toward the appropriate shifts in thinking.

**Reflect**

Write an astronomical sum up on the board. Explain that the figure represents the amount of money lost in the deals that fell through as a result of the groups' ineffective initial contacts. Then distribute a synthetic million-dollar bill to each member of the group and say, "Now this reflects your subsequent financial success as a result of your newly perfected greeting skills." Conclude this part of the training with an account of a personal experience in which a friendly greeting you extended to a seatmate on a flight to Hawaii resulted in a five-million-dollar sale (or your own version of a related story).

# The Bricks and Mortar of the TrainSmart Model

This section introduces ten fundamental aspects of the TrainSmart approach to training. It is divided into two parts. First, we'll look at five critical beliefs that comprise the building blocks of the model—the "bricks." Then we'll examine five guiding principles of effective training that hold it all together—the "mortar." These beliefs and principles are the foundation of the TrainSmart model. Let's review them one brick at a time.

## 1. Teach People, Not Content

Undeniably, content is important. After all, it's the primary reason why companies invest in training. However, TrainSmart recognizes

**Figure 1.2** The Bricks of the TrainSmart Model

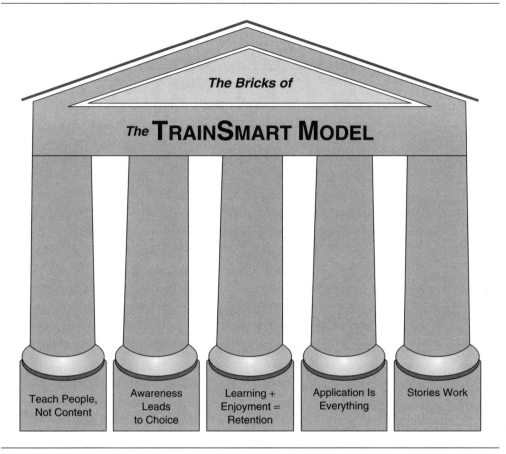

that content means very little outside a *human* context. It's based on the idea that learners are, first and foremost, *people*, and *their* needs come first. The point is, people simply won't learn until we truly take their needs into account. If we are sensitive to the needs of the group and respect each individual, we will foster the type of safe and trusting environment that supports optimal learning.

To teach people, not content, we must ensure they

- are physically and socially comfortable;
- can see how the content is relevant to their life and work; and
- feel emotionally safe.

Maintaining a focus on *people first* requires us to shift our thinking away from the traditional view of learning where "pupils" listen to

## GOOD TEACHERS ARE ALWAYS LEARNING FROM THEIR STUDENTS.

their "teacher." In other words, we don't teach *to* people, we teach *with* them. Training *to* a group assumes instruction happens only in one direction—from the trainer to the participants. Training *with* a group acknowledges that learning is bilateral—it's an exchange between individuals. Thus the TrainSmart framework acknowledges that the trainer's viewpoint is not the *only* valid one.

### 2. Awareness Leads to Choice

*Given all they know, people always make the best choice available to them.*

This statement introduces the idea that our job as trainers is to give participants additional "choices." The way participants choose to approach a problem will depend on the number of ways they are *aware* the problem can be tackled. If they are aware of only one approach, that's the one they'll use.

Consider the analogy of a tool kit. If we have only a hammer, we'll try to use it to solve every carpentry task. But if someone gives us a screwdriver and shows us how to use it, we'll get a lot better at putting in screws!

When we teach, we broaden the range of choices participants have by making them aware they have other options. In other words, we add to their "skills tool kit" by showing them new ideas and how to apply them.

This idea is important to us as teachers. It focuses us on the fundamental point that if participants have an alternative way of doing something that seems better to them—or that they are more comfortable with—they will choose this. Therefore, if we want them to learn to do something differently, we must demonstrate the usefulness of the new approach and show how it complements their existing skills.

## 3. Learning + Enjoyment = Retention

Cognitive scientists agree that emotions have a significant effect on our recall. Think about it: what do you remember from your own childhood? If you're like most people, your most durable memories fall into one of two distinct categories: times of great pleasure or great pain.

As trainers, we rarely use negative emotions to influence recall—unless, of course, we're running a boot camp! However, we can greatly improve participants' recall by connecting content with positive emotions by using humor, joy, and playful interaction within our training.

For example, instead of teaching a concept by merely talking about it, try introducing participants to its relevance using an intriguing interactive exercise. You'll find many of these illustrated throughout the book.

A word of warning: we need to handle people's emotions *carefully*. For example, many people may have had bad experiences with humor in the teaching environment. While people love to laugh at a joke, they don't want to *be* one.

So be sure to keep playful interactions meaningful and work to create a learning environment based on emotional safety and mutual respect. Then you can use positive emotions to help participants make deep and powerful connections with the content. Think back to your childhood: did you ever truly master anything that you didn't enjoy?

# WHAT WE LEARN WITH **PLEASURE,** WE NEVER FORGET.

### 4. Application Is Everything

Learners need to apply new knowledge to their own, unique situations. Demonstrating the validity or usefulness of the knowledge through association with concrete examples and real-life encounters not only helps participants understand and apply the content, it also helps them remember it!

*Nothing is taught if nothing is learned.*
*And nothing is learned if nothing is applied.*

You can show participants how to apply content through small-group exercises, games, case studies, brain twisters, and role plays. Facilitating such interactions frequently helps participants understand how to use their new knowledge.

I sometimes open a lesson by posing a problem. I might say, "Please help me identify what's wrong with the following situation." In this case, the application becomes the starting point of the presentation. Then we look at variations on the problem and discuss ways to address it.

## 5. Stories Work

Long before there were books or movies or computers, there were stories—metaphorical tales that acted as the repository of a culture's collective wisdom. The storytellers of ancient communities were among the most revered and venerated of citizens, because civilizations depended on the verbal tradition of passing knowledge to the next generation. Today, stories remain a powerful means of transferring knowledge. Good trainers use them all the time when sharing case studies, personal experiences, news articles, metaphors, and jokes.

All of these story devices can teach us something about the world, while simultaneously triggering our emotions, tapping into our unconscious, and stimulating visual images that foster recall. Of course, we can always use more stories—and you'll find some at the back of this book. But remember: our own lives are full of potential parables—all we need to do is see through the eyes of a storyteller.

Now let's take a look at the principles that hold the bricks of the TrainSmart model together.

## 1. Crest of the Wave

Way out in the distance, a swell begins to build. It is slow and steady at first, gradually gaining height and momentum as it moves ever closer to shore. Arching to a crest, the wave reaches critical mass, peaks, and crashes down over itself. The water rolls forward and finally dissipates as it washes up on the sandy shore. This is the natural rhythm of the learning process in the training room.

Simply put, much like waves building, peaking, then crashing down, there are swells, crests, and tumbles in the training environment. When learners reach the end of their ability to draw useful information from a given mode of instruction, they reach the *crest of the wave*. At this point, we need to change the manner of instruction to refocus their interest and attention.

This means we need to observe and listen to the room. What is the sound level? Are participants on or off task? Are they sitting on the edge of their seats or rocking back and forth in them? What is the energy level? Is it time for a change of pace? Do learners need to move around or take a break? These are questions we must ask ourselves moment by moment. If we ignore these vital cues, participants may grow increasingly uncomfortable, hesitant, and resistant.

The point is: training is a dynamic art. We need to be constantly responsive to the waves of interest in the room, stay present in the moment, and respond to the energy and reactions of the participants.

**Figure 1.3**     The Mortar of the TrainSmart Model

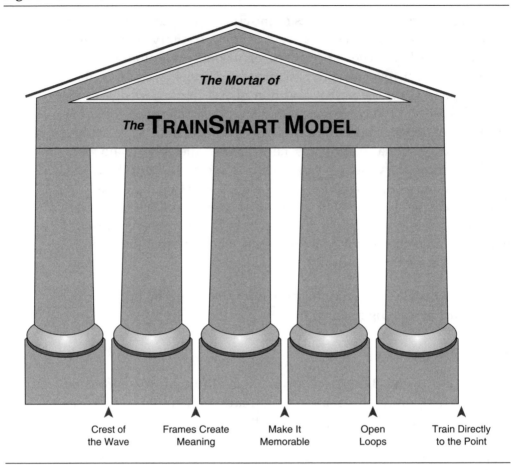

Crest of | Frames Create | Make It | Open | Train Directly
the Wave | Meaning | Memorable | Loops | to the Point

Even when the many environmental factors that impact a training session are perfect—the room temperature, furniture arrangement, and type of equipment—the question still remains . . .

*How long can participants effectively pay attention?*

While answers will always vary among individuals and situations, my experience is that adults can fully pay attention in a new learning situation for only about fifteen minutes at a time. In fact, if we expect participants to sit still for too long, they quickly become tired and find it hard to focus.

So what does this mean to us as trainers?

It means we need to provide strategic brief energy breaks in the form of mental or physical "state changes" about every fifteen minutes—or sooner if we sense the room beginning to "crest." To do that, it helps to think of each session as a menu with hors d'oeuvres, a main course, and dessert. Between courses, provide state changes and movement activities to avoid overloading participants with information.

It is vital not to overload participants. Given the volume of information trainers have to deliver, it's tempting to continue to speak past the point where participants can effectively absorb new content. Instead, once the wave crests, we need to allow participants the time to process new information through a variety of modalities (talking, reading, editing notes, brainstorming, or watching a video). This sets up a win-win situation: on the one hand, participants make connections and consolidate information for long-term memory; on the other, we trainers can assess learning progress—not to mention taking a break ourselves!

As a result, everyone comes back refreshed and refocused. This is what *training smarter* is all about.

*If you're not riding the crest of the wave,*
*chances are you may find yourself beneath it.*

## 2. Frames Create Meaning

Consider the following scenario. A trainer introduces an exercise with only one brief remark, "Welcome to The Maze! Here's how the game is played." He then explains how to play the game, but learners are skeptical and hesitant about participating. Why might this happen?

On closer inspection, we can see the trainer did not effectively *frame* the activity. Learners are busy wondering: why should we do this? What's the point? How does this relate to me, the topic, or my work? Without a frame, participants understandably decide the activity is irrelevant and turn their attention elsewhere.

The next day, the trainer decides to try a different approach. He introduces the activity to a new group like this: "Welcome to The Maze! The Maze is a puzzle. As we solve it, some issues may emerge that we can talk about later as a group and learn from."

With this frame, participants are able to grasp the learning purpose and significance of the exercise. They prepare themselves for the activity and the discussion to follow. The frame has successfully provided meaning.

### 3. Make It Memorable

We need to present material in a way that helps participants to remember it easily and naturally. This sounds self-evident, but the problem is that our own familiarity with the material gives us the edge in creating a memory strategy suitable for retaining it. Learners, on the other hand, must first *comprehend* the new material before they can remember it.

You'll find memory strategies throughout *TrainSmart*, but here's a quick synopsis.

We've already talked about the value of storytelling and engaging emotions. In addition, you can help learners remember important concepts by linking the concepts with images or with mnemonic strategies, such as acrostics and acronyms.

For example, the acronym HOMES has helped many U.S. children learn the names of America's five Great Lakes: Huron, Ontario, Michigan, Erie, and Superior. Similarly, almost every American youngster, for example, has learned the alphabet to the tune of "Twinkle, Twinkle, Little Star." While primarily used today by younger learners, mnemonic techniques work with people of all ages. Everyone remembers more when the brain is provided with additional connections and cues.

Another memory strategy you'll discover in *TrainSmart* is *involving* participants in the learning, rather than *telling* them about it. You can involve people through discussion, role plays or exercises that allow participants to "discover" the content themselves. Or you can involve them in the teaching process itself.

*If you really want to know something, teach it.*

Asking participants to teach or lead aspects of the training is a highly effective technique for enhancing recall. Even getting participants to share their level of prior learning or experience with the subject early in the training will engage and stimulate recall by building on prior knowledge.

Finally, one of the best things you can do to help participants remember is to limit your content to what is digestible in the allotted time. Remember: when the wave crests, people stop learning.

Before you finalize your training plan, ask yourself the question: how memorable is it?

## 4. Open Loops

It was the first morning of a two-day technical training seminar. Participants were learning to repair a new walkie-talkie that would soon be sold in stores. At the start of the session, the trainer passed out a walkie-talkie to each person. When all the participants had received one, she asked that they turn them on. None of the units worked. She then said, "Each device has some sort of problem: I personally saw to that. Now, here's a twenty dollar bill. If you can fix your walkie-talkie, or anyone's around you in the next five minutes, the money is yours. Your five-minute countdown begins now."

The trainees launched into the repair process—taking their walkie-talkies apart, interacting with others around them, and problem solving. When the five-minute time period was up, none of the units had been repaired. "OK," said the trainer, "now let's learn how to make some money fixing these things." All eyes were on her, and it was clear that she had successfully employed the powerful training strategy known as an *open loop.*

An open loop is any statement, action, visual device, or other event that gives participants foreknowledge of what is coming.

Trainers use open loops to set the stage for what is about to happen, elicit curiosity, and build suspense.

There are many ways to achieve this effect. You can do it with visuals, such as signs or posters placed around the room, or with a message displayed on the board or screen. A guitar placed in plain view, but not mentioned, can serve as an open loop until it is used later. Or perhaps you might leave a box in plain view with a variety of colorful supplies poking out. You can use any event that arouses anticipation to create an open loop.

Open loops are wonderful training devices because they create a dynamic that participants find irresistible: they need to "close the loop." Consider this metaphor: have you ever been in a car listening to one of your favorite songs when, just before it ends, the DJ fades it out or begins speaking over the ending? Isn't that annoying? What annoys us is that the loop doesn't close. The longer we listen to the song, the stronger the loop becomes, and the more dissatisfaction we feel when it is cut short. Once a loop has been opened, it is human nature to want to close it.

Open loops have universal appeal. They form the plot of most fictional best sellers and are exploited by advertisers. For example, colorful advertisements for exotic destinations can create the desire to travel; the only way to close the loop is to book a vacation.

While open loops come in many shapes and colors, their common denominator is that they alert participants to what is coming and its potential value. This both focuses their attention on receiving the new information and helps them remember it.

A couple of warnings: using loops can be an effective component of your learning strategy, but they are never the entire strategy. Most important, remember that when you open a loop, you've eventually got to close it!

## 5. Train Directly to the Point

A *little* knowledge, as the saying goes, can be a dangerous thing. In the training setting, however, *a lot* of knowledge can be an *even more* dangerous thing. Why? Because we forget one of the basic rules of effective instruction: *train directly to the point!* So limit your information with a simple question: does it support participants in understanding the topic? If it doesn't, no matter how entertaining or interesting, it probably doesn't need to be there. The following example illustrates this important principle.

The class was billed as an introduction to the company's revised e-mail system. It was geared toward staff members who had little or no experience working with the new program. The trainer was a young man who had been working with computers for most of his life. As participants filed in, he guided each of them to a computer station.

"I'd like to start by saying that using this program is really easy. You'll get the hang of it in no time at all, and pretty soon you'll be able to move right on to some of the more interesting aspects of it, such as creating multiple client lists you can simultaneously e-mail, creating a personalized signature, and building databases where you can cross reference the critical needs of some of our important companies. Why, you can even . . ."

However, by this point he had already lost the attention of most of the participants. Although he spoke with enthusiasm, they were intimidated and unfamiliar with the trainer's language. He had intended to create a sense of excitement in the room. However, by introducing too much new information too rapidly, he had unintentionally created the opposite effect.

After the lack of success in his first session, the trainer decided to make some changes. The next time the training was conducted, he

was better prepared and decided to use the principle of *training directly to the point*. The first thing he said was, "Welcome. Thank you for coming. Please begin by opening the new e-mail program on your computer. Here's how that's done . . . "

At this point, he waited patiently while participants located the appropriate icon. It took a little time, but finally everyone had the new program open and running on their computer. Next he showed them how to send a message, and asked that they all send one to him. When this had been successfully accomplished, he had them send a brief message to each other, and showed them how to send a reply. He continued like this throughout the session, at each point introducing only what the participants needed to know, and not moving forward until everyone had successfully completed each step. In the end, 100 percent of participants achieved the course objectives!

How were the original and revised approaches different? In the revised approach, the trainer took into account the needs and experience levels of the participants, and geared the instruction accordingly. The bottom line? Avoid the temptation to add unnecessary information: *train directly to the point*.

## A Sample TrainSmart Schedule

### Morning Session (Part 1)

- **Arrival:** Have upbeat music playing as participants enter the training area and get themselves settled.

- **Welcome and Greet:** Create involvement through various activities in which participants meet each other.

- **Content Introduction:** Introduce the colorful posters on the walls and have participants take a quick trip around the room to review them. The posters should reflect the key concepts of the training.

- **Opening Parable:** Tell a story that sets the scene or mood for the day. For example, you might share "The Traveler" (see parables in Part Three) to symbolize the importance of being open to new ideas and not rushing to judgment.

- **Distribution of Resources:** Before the training begins, hide the workbooks somewhere in the room. Now have participants "gather their first gem" by standing up and finding a workbook. This activity doubles as a state-changer and as a way to get the blood moving a little bit.

- **Plant an Open Loop:** Mention to participants that they might surprise themselves before the day is done. Hint that something intriguing will happen after lunch.
- **First Exploration:** Introduce/frame the activity before you begin.
- **Debriefing:** Ask the participants to write down at least three emotions they experienced while engaged in the exploration activity. Afterward, ask for volunteers to share their ideas. Record these ideas on a flip-chart.

–Morning Break–

### Morning Session (Part 2)

- **Engager:** Bring participants back and refocus their attention with a brief two-minute energizer.
- **Second Exploration:** Introduce/frame the activity.
- **Application:** Have participants pair up and consider how they might apply the learning to their work or home lives. Subsequent to the pair share, regroup and ask participants to share their responses while you once again record them on a flip-chart page.
- **Make It Memorable:** Give participants the last five minutes of the morning to make notes about the most important concepts they've learned and how they might apply them personally and professionally.

–Lunch Break–

### Afternoon Session (Part 1)

- **Engager:** Engage learners physically with a brief activity that is mildly active and encourages social interaction.
- **Close Open Loop:** Remind participants about the intriguing after-lunch activity, and then tell them they—not you—will be teaching the rest of the session.
- **Exploration:** Have participants meet in small groups. Provide each group with an index card describing a pertinent concept learned in the morning session and with instructions for planning a five-minute lesson based on that concept. Allow a set period of time in which to plan and practice the lesson they will be presenting to the rest of the group.

–Afternoon Break–

*(Continued)*

(Continued)

**Afternoon Session (Part 2)**

- **Final Energizer:** Have learners create and post "mind maps" related to the material they've been learning.
- **Application:** Have the groups present their five-minute lessons.
- **Debriefing:** After the presentations, ask the class to provide feedback about what they felt worked and what didn't. This is also the time when the various pieces of the training are pulled together for a final recap.
- **Review:** Have participants stand up and review all of the posters on the walls. Provide index cards for them to record any final questions that they have. This is also a good time for participants to answer each other's questions as they walk around and discuss the posters and mind maps.
- **Ownership:** Ask everyone to complete a session evaluation that focuses on what they felt they received the most value from, and that elicits ideas for how the course could be made even better in the future.
- **Closing Parable:** End with a story that reinforces your underlying theme. For example, you might tell the "Animal School" parable (see parables in Part Three) to reinforce the importance of training to an individual's strengths as opposed to forcing a square peg into a round hole. We all have natural gifts, we just need to recognize and strengthen them.
- **Closing Remarks:** Play some upbeat, inspiring music as you thank and acknowledge participants for their energy, enthusiasm, and attention.

This hypothetical training schedule demonstrates how the TrainSmart model looks in practice. Certainly, there are thousands of ways to translate the principles and/or modify them. The bottom line? *Engage, Frame, Explore, Debrief, and Reflect!*

# PART TWO

# Twenty-Five Key Concepts for Training Smarter

**TrainSmart Key Concept Matrix: The Twenty-Five Key Concepts**

1. Acknowledgment
2. Bridges and Zones
3. Comfort Levels
4. Task Completion
5. Contrast
6. Precise Directions
7. Resource Distribution
8. Teach It Standing
9. Participant Inquiry
10. Adequate Response Time
11. Specify Response Mode
12. Question/Clarify/Question
13. Managing Disruptions
14. Creative Note-Taking
15. Positive Language
16. Involve, Don't Tell

*(Continued)*

(Continued)

17. Ownership
18. Pause for Visuals
19. Press and Release
20. Purposeful Body Language
21. Visual-Field Variations
22. Vocal Italics
23. Music Matters
24. Guiding Attention
25. Verbal Specificity

# TrainSmart Key Concept Matrix: The Twenty-Five Key Concepts

You'll find most of TrainSmart's Key Concepts useful throughout your training. However, some of them are particularly important in certain phases of the training cycle. The matrix below highlights when you should be most aware of them when creating your training plan.

| Key Concept | Engage | Frame | Explore | Debrief | Reflect |
|---|---|---|---|---|---|
| Acknowledgment | | | ◆ | | ◆ |
| Bridges and Zones | ◆ | | ◆ | ◆ | |
| Comfort Levels | ◆ | ◆ | ◆ | | |
| Task Completion | | | ◆ | | ◆ |
| Contrast | ◆ | | | ◆ | ◆ |
| Precise Directions | ◆ | | ◆ | ◆ | |
| Resource Distribution | ◆ | | ◆ | | |
| Teach It Standing | ◆ | | ◆ | ◆ | |
| Participant Inquiry | ◆ | ◆ | | | |
| Adequate Response Time | | | | ◆ | ◆ |
| Specify Response Mode | | ◆ | | ◆ | |
| Question/Clarify/Question | | | | ◆ | ◆ |
| Managing Disruptions | | | Whenever they arise! | | |
| Creative Note-Taking | | | ◆ | ◆ | ◆ |
| Positive Language | | | All the time! | | |
| Involve, Don't Tell | | | ◆ | | |
| Ownership | ◆ | ◆ | | | ◆ |
| Pause for Visuals | | | ◆ | ◆ | |
| Press and Release | ◆ | | ◆ | ◆ | |
| Purposeful Body Language | | ◆ | ◆ | ◆ | |
| Visual-Field Variations | | | Frequently! | | |
| Vocal Italics | | ◆ | ◆ | ◆ | |
| Guiding Attention | | ◆ | | ◆ | |
| Verbal Specificity | | ◆ | ◆ | ◆ | |

# Key Concept 1

# Acknowledgment

## What It Is

*Acknowledgment*—the art of recognizing and affirming achievement—is an important aspect of promoting learning. Think about it: when your own efforts are positively acknowledged or affirmed by others, doesn't your motivation soar? At the very least, it makes you feel good. And if participants "feel good," they will be more open to learning and more likely to attach content to positive emotions, which will help them to remember.

## Why It's Important

Consistently encouraging participants by acknowledging their efforts, regardless of the results of those efforts, is essential to the learning process. Consider the image of a sailboat out on the open water. Imagine what happens to it as it encounters heavy seas. If the boat has steady winds to push it along, it can handle those seas, but if the wind is inconsistent and swings around wildly, the boat will be in trouble. In a training room, the same idea applies. Steady encouragement will keep your participants moving forward, even in the face of strong resistance or challenging circumstances. By contrast, if acknowledgment is inconsistent—or worse, if participants are ignored or reprimanded for their best efforts, the "ship of learning" can be thrown off course. The ideal learning and training environment is when the ship of learning encounters a steady breeze of encouragement to fill its sails.

## How to Incorporate It

The best way to create a steady breeze of encouragement is to use multiple forms of acknowledgment. This acknowledgment must be genuine, focused on an individual's specific efforts, and provided frequently enough to keep learners on course.

That means we, as trainers, need to respond positively and with enthusiasm to a solicited answer—even if it wasn't exactly what we were looking for. This includes many situations, such as thanking individuals for their responses, congratulating pairs for completing role plays, and acknowledging groups when they have completed an assigned task.

However, this trainer-to-participant flow of reward and praise, although useful, rarely gives participants the frequency of acknowledgment they need—especially when the ratio of learners to trainer is high. To achieve that frequency, we need to spread the responsibility for acknowledgment to include participants by setting up opportunities for positive peer reviews and encouraging peer support at all times.

Encouraging participant-to-participant acknowledgment helps involve participants more deeply in the learning and creates a more dynamic (and hence more effective) learning environment; it also lessens the trainer's load.

Here are a few acknowledgment strategies to consider when designing your next training program. These are just a handful of possibilities—you'll find many other opportunities for participant-to-participant acknowledgment in your particular training activities.

### Self-Acknowledgment

Ask participants to assess their own learning by completing a questionnaire or survey on a recent topic. However, avoid presenting it as any sort of "test" that participants could "fail." Instead, emphasize its role as a feedback mechanism for learners to assess their own strengths and weaknesses and to increase their understanding.

### Peer Acknowledgment

Compliments between participants go a long way toward building learner confidence. So, whenever participants work together, encourage them to acknowledge each other for their contributions to the team. For example, after completing an activity, you can encourage learners to review each other's work and identify the positive aspects of it.

### Physical Acknowledgment

A physical acknowledgment, like a handshake or a high five, can be a powerful means of acknowledging others' efforts. This simple technique for quickly giving peer acknowledgment is especially effective when the group has been engaged in a physical activity.

## When to Use It

We need to use acknowledgment as often as possible. That means looking beyond the obvious moments when participants succeed or give what we think is the "right" answer.

The most important time to provide acknowledgment is when participants achieve small successes or make honest endeavors that nevertheless fall short of mastery. Regardless of results, *honest effort* itself is commendable. After all, it's the only way some people will master anything—so we need to encourage it. If we reward honest effort with steady encouragement and positive feedback, participants will try again—perhaps even harder. They will also be more likely to stay mentally, physically, and emotionally involved—which is essential for mastering any new and challenging task.

## When *Not* to Use It

While it's important to *consistently* acknowledge the efforts of learners throughout a training, doing so excessively can reduce the impact of this technique. If we provide *constant* praise, learners may perceive it as contrived or disingenuous. They may even become distracted and annoyed, which could break the cycle of learning. However, don't miss the opportunity to acknowledge any participant exerting honest effort in a learning activity, regardless of the result.

---

### A Real-Life Training Example

The setting is a weeklong training for people who have been with the organization for at least five years and are looking to move into management. As the training winds down, participants are given a questionnaire. The final question is baffling. It asks, "What's the name of the head custodian responsible for the building that houses our organization?"

Most of the participants are stumped. Since the question appears to be random, most of them decide it must be a joke and leave it unanswered. When everyone has completed the assessment, someone asks the trainer whether the final question was important. He replies, "Definitely! Success comes not just from *what* you know, it also depends on *who* you know. In your lifetime you will meet many people. Each of them is significant and deserves your attention, even if all you do is smile and say hello."

The trainer in this situation was attempting to broaden participants' horizons as to the power and importance of acknowledging *everyone*'s contribution at work. His point was that this heightened awareness of the value others bring could be valuable in a many situations—certainly professionally, and perhaps even personally.

---

Hey, well done . . . you've just completed Key Concept 1!

*My thoughts about applying this concept:*

_____

_____

_____

_____

_____

_____

_____

# Key Concept 2

# Bridges and Zones

## What It Is

*Bridges* and *zones* provide participants with cognitive and emotional connections that help them learn. They set expectations for the type of instruction that is about to happen and guide participants into an appropriate state of learning readiness.

*Zones* are physical locations in the learning environment that we can use—much like actors use areas on a stage—to stimulate participants' unconscious expectations. The three most common zones are shown in Figure 2.1.

*Bridges* are the connections from these zones to our learners. We create them by intentionally altering our tone of voice and gestures as we move to a new zone and a different mode of learning. Figure 2.1 also shows the way to create a bridge from each zone to our participants.

1.  The *instructional zone* is the area nearest the screen or whiteboard—the space farthest from the participants—where we deliver content and use most of our visuals. When you move to this location, participants know that new information is about to be presented and that it's time to focus their attention, organize materials, and prepare to take notes.

2.  The *facilitation zone* is closer to the participants—a space from which you can interact with them more casually. You can use this zone to respond to participants' questions or when soliciting answers from them. When you shift to this area, learners immediately expect

**Figure 2.1**    Bridges and Zones

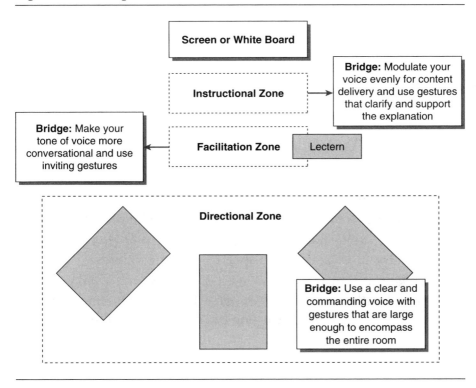

a different level of interaction and adjust their thinking accordingly. For example, they start mentally preparing to think about and answer questions on the material just presented.

3. The *directional zone* is the area closest to the participants (or even among them). Here's where you give instructions or mobilize the group. Being this close to participants as you move among them will intensify the impact of your information.

## Why It's Important

Bridges and zones set the stage for learning, create a constructive and focused climate, trigger positive emotions, and provide smooth transitions from one task to another. Importantly, they also help us create a predictable learning environment. Just as children depend on regular schedules and rituals, adult learners find comfort in them too. By giving participants predictable cues for transitioning to another mode of learning, we provide a sense of security, thereby freeing up the brain for learning.

## How to Incorporate It

- To create a sense of relaxation and emotional safety at the start of your training, consider using the *facilitation zone* to initiate casual conversation and interaction between you and your participants. Maintain a relaxed posture and informal tone of voice.
- Establish your zones early in the workshop and be consistent in the way you use them. Don't wait, for example, until the workshop is half over to start using the facilitation zone.
- Use each zone at least three times to make participants familiar with the areas and their respective learning modes.
- Make the transition from one zone to the other smooth and casual, rather than abrupt or overt. Practice switching from one zone and its mode of learning to another before the training.

## When to Use It

Try to shift between zones

- at the beginning of a session when establishing rapport;
- when you change learning mode;
- at the close of a session;
- when providing important instructions;
- when making a critical point; and
- when soliciting audience participation.

Using bridges and zones clearly, deliberately, and consistently throughout your training can make a world of difference to learning readiness.

## When *Not* to Use It

As you practice using the bridges and zones concept, you'll see the key is to use the strategy *consistently*. If we wander around the room unconsciously between zones, for example, we give the learner permission to wander (mentally) as well.

The more purposeful our delivery, the more we focus participants on acquiring the information. To be effective, use bridges and zones in a well-planned, consistent, and purposeful way.

## A Real-Life Training Example

It's the start of a two-day corporate workshop in which teamwork is the primary focus. All the participants have arrived and the trainer is ready to begin. She signals the group by casually approaching an unoccupied desk near the front row. Sitting comfortably on the edge of the desk, she says, "Good morning. Welcome to today's workshop. I'd like to begin by providing an opportunity for us to get acquainted with one another. As we go around the room, let's introduce ourselves to the group and share why we're here. Feel free to share any experiences, good or bad, in which teamwork has played an important role in your personal or professional life."

The participants and the trainer spend a few minutes introducing themselves, and sharing their thoughts and experiences. The trainer thanks the group and heads back toward the whiteboard. As she points to some text written on the whiteboard, she says, "Now let's focus on the five key principles of effective teamwork. These principles will form the framework for everything we learn today, so you may want to take notes."

The trainer is effectively leading the group's focus as she uses bridges and moves between zones to make a smooth transition from one learning mode to the next. Learners unconsciously follow her lead, becoming more and more comfortable as the trainer demonstrates an expert command of the audience and learning environment. She has successfully established an initial level of connection between the zone she is using and the mode of instruction within that zone.

*My thoughts about applying this concept:*

---

---

---

---

---

---

---

# Key Concept 3

# Comfort Levels

## What It Is

Maintaining *comfort levels* means paying careful attention to the physical and emotional concerns of learners during activities that require them to interact with one another. This may sound like a tall order when we consider the extent to which interpersonal skills, social and cultural norms, and comfort levels can greatly vary among individuals. However, despite these differences, we can incorporate a host of techniques to help people feel safe in the learning environment.

## Why It's Important

Interactive exercises can potentially create physical and psychological discomfort among participants; if not handled with the utmost respect and sensitivity, this can lead to a breakdown in learning. While this may seem obvious, it should never be taken lightly. When students are even slightly uncomfortable, their enthusiasm and cooperation decrease rapidly. In extreme cases, they may even rebel. However, if we create an environment where participants can relax and feel emotionally at ease, bonds of trust will develop quickly between trainer and participants, and among participants themselves, allowing us to stretch the boundaries of learning.

## How to Incorporate It

Here are some techniques you can use to establish a sense of safety in the learning environment.

- Always give participants the permission to "pass" if they wish on any aspect of an exercise or activity.
- Always establish ground rules before starting an exercise (i.e., when it's appropriate to ask questions or give feedback, time expectations, transition instructions).
- Provide a road map of the exercise before starting, so learners know what to expect.
- Be sensitive to how groups are organized/selected. Everyone should always feel included. For example, in most situations where groups are formed, we should preferably allow them to decide who will be in their group. However, if you notice one or more of the participants not "fitting in" with everyone else, try to find a way to control how groups are formed so these individuals are naturally included. One option might be to ask the whole group to count off by fours, and then split them by numbers so the ones are all together, and so on.
- If a group activity requires a leader or other facilitation roles, organize your method for establishing them prior to the activity and with sensitivity to involving everyone.
- Establish trust incrementally between trainer and participants before plunging into potentially emotional situations. Start with gentle, nonthreatening activities and progress to more challenging ones as trust is established.
- Preface activities that might potentially bring up strong emotions with an acknowledgment that it is "okay" to move through them in whatever way emerges. Have tissues readily available for exercises that might elicit tears.
- If the setting is not appropriate for people to express strong emotions—and in many business environments it is not—avoid activities that may stimulate them.
- Always debrief an exercise at the end. This allows participants to deal with any unresolved questions or concerns and provides some closure on the experience.
- Many people feel uncomfortable closing their eyes in large group settings. Minimize activities that require learners to do this until trust has been established, and initially limit the time to approximately ten seconds. Always provide the option of doing the activity without eyes closed.
- When an activity requires invading the normal boundaries of personal space, be sensitive to the distress that this can cause

some individuals. Watch participants carefully for signs of stress and adjust the physical parameters of the exercise if necessary.

- When an activity requires participants to sit in pairs facing each other, the arrangement can quickly turn awkward. Watch for signs of discomfort or idle conversation, and provide participants with a reason to turn away from each other in such instances. Give pairs instructions about what to do once they've completed the task (i.e., move on to the next one, take a break, sit down).

- Don't put learners on the spot unless there is a clear, productive reason for doing so. Learners who feel embarrassed or threatened will not have the focus necessary to listen and learn.

- Always acknowledge or apologize to a participant in private should an unexpected, embarrassing, or uncomfortable situation occur. Let participants know you care about their feelings.

## When to Use It

While ensuring the physical and psychological comfort of participants should always be a priority, perhaps the most important time to use this concept is during group activities—especially physical ones that require touching and close contact. Such exercises intensify the potential for discomfort for many learners, often because they fear looking foolish in front of their peers or because they have had bad past experiences in similar situations.

## When *Not* to Use It

Occasionally (depending on the nature of the training), we purposefully want learners to experience the tension and bodily sensations of "fear" or "anxiety." However, even in rare cases like this, we need to take precautions so learners know they have a choice and the freedom not to participate. Thus, even in these situations, we still need to lay the groundwork for "comfort" and safety to create a foundation of trust.

---

### A Real-Life Training Example

In a workshop on teamwork, the trainer was leading an exercise commonly known as The Human Knot, in which clusters of participants join hands randomly, creating a tangled knot of arms. The task is to figure out how to untangle the knot while staying connected to each other. After asking the groups to join hands, the trainer announced the following: "I bet you're all wondering what you're about to do! Well, actually, this activity is called The Human Knot! But before we begin, let me tell you a little bit about its background." The trainer then launched into a three-minute history of the activity.

What's wrong with this picture? The problem, although probably obvious to you, was not so obvious to this trainer. Introducing the exercise while participants were left standing in awkward positions, holding sweaty hands with someone they didn't know, did not enhance the participants' sense of emotional safety and comfort. Not surprisingly, it wasn't long before the participants released each other's hands and the exercise lost momentum. Worse still, the participants—now slightly embarrassed or impatient—were less inclined to trust the trainer in future activities.

*My thoughts about applying this concept:*

_____

_____

_____

_____

_____

_____

_____

# Key Concept 4

# Task Completion

## What It Is

*Task completion* creates a sense of closure before moving from one topic to the next. It both helps embed the previous learning and gives the brain a little time to prepare for transition to the next topic. Just as you might give a youngster a warning that the TV will go off in five minutes, we need to prepare adult learners for the next step in the learning schedule before arriving there. We also need to deal with any lingering issues, questions, or concerns from the previous activity that might otherwise distract individuals and divide their attention.

## Why It's Important

Most of us have experienced a training or seminar that felt disjointed, awkward, or even frustrating, without being able to put a finger on why. In contrast, when a lesson is well planned and includes task completion and smooth transitions, learners glide through the process easily and naturally. Therefore, as trainers, we need to plan actively how to make each session flow from one stage to the next.

This means keeping participants aware of where the current activity fits into the session flow. For example, when presenting an exercise or activity to a group, always explain what your time expectations are, what learners should do when they're finished, and what the following agenda item will be. Afterward, debrief the group and answer any remaining questions or concerns. This process reinforces important conclusions and provides closure while also developing interest in the next step of the learning process.

## How to Incorporate It

Whether completing a single topic, a task, or an entire training session, keep the following key elements in mind:

- *Closures* and *task completions* can range from a simple, one-sentence instruction to a complex set of activities and rituals. But completion is so crucial to meaningful learning that it's worth setting aside at least 10 percent of your entire presentation for this purpose. Even if you're rushed or running out of time, don't omit this important part of learning. If your presentation is ten minutes, your closure should be at least a few minutes. If you're doing a fifty-minute presentation, conduct your closure in the last five to eight minutes. By contrast, a one-day training might have a closure that is twenty to thirty minutes in length.

- Write down in one or two succinct sentences the primary goal(s) of the exercise or activity. Then make sure these are among your final words when you close the learning session. Since our attention bias is strongest at both the beginning and the end of a session, it's a good idea to take advantage of learners' expanded memory capacity during these windows.

- Focus learners' attention on a sense of accomplishment. Participants are more ready to leave a learning segment if they feel they've learned something new and useful. If they don't have this sense of "cognitive gain," participants will be less likely to "follow" as you lead them through the next learning task. Instead, they'll still be wondering about the relevance of the previous session—and not concentrating on the next topic.

- If participants are to remember new learning, they must *internalize* it—a concept also known as a "self-convincing" state. In other words, participants not only need to understand the concept in principle, they also need to know how it applies specifically to them and believe it. Closings, therefore, are most effective when they help the learner *embody* and apply new concepts to themselves.

## Closing Questions to Focus on Accomplishment and Internalize Learning

- What did I learn?
- How does what I just learned apply to me or the circumstances in my life, now or in the future?
- How much of the lesson (in percentage terms or on a scale of one to ten) did I follow and understand?

- Where might there be holes in my understanding?
- How might this new skill/information benefit me personally/ professionally?
- What memory tool might help me remember what I've learned today?
- How do I feel about what I've learned?

Even simple instructions require task completion. For example, when you invite participants to raise their hands, remember to tell them to put them down. While this instruction may seem unnecessary, it's amazing how often participants wait for it! Similarly, when inviting participants to take a deep breath, be sure to instruct them to exhale as well. Again, this may seem an unnecessary step, but many training participants have been seen patiently holding their breath while waiting for a cue from the facilitator to exhale.

When closing a multiple-day session, or when disbanding for a break, be sure to inform participants of what they can expect when they return. Unless there is a specific structural reason *not* to do so, prepare learners for what's ahead.

Since people work and think at different speeds, always provide adequate time for most (if not all) participants to complete an activity. While we can't always give every participant time to fully accomplish a task, we can be careful not to cram too many learning goals into a single session. Teaching too much information in a limited time frame rushes everyone through the learning process and bombards participants with more content than they can reasonably digest in the time allotted.

## When to Use It

At the very least, initiate a final closing exercise or activity after almost every learning session—whether it's an hour-long, day-long, or multiday training. In addition, use closing rituals between learning segments to clear the air for the next topic. Perhaps the most important time to emphasize completion is at the conclusion of an entire training—this is an important time to tie all the loose ends together and relate the parts to the whole. This simple act can dramatically reinforce recall.

## When *Not* to Use It

There are occasions when we might purposefully leave an activity or exercise unclosed. For example, we might want learners to brainstorm ideas overnight or assimilate a concept on their own before drawing conclusions about it later. When used sparingly and purposefully, this can be a good strategy for stimulating critical analysis. However, for the most part, learners won't tolerate lack of closure for very long.

---

## A Real-Life Training Example

Be careful not to leave learners hanging at any given stage of an exercise or activity. The following example reflects how an uncompleted action can leave some learners in an uncomfortable position and negatively impact the learning of the entire group.

At the front of the training room, a large piece of paper is taped to the wall, stretching from floor to ceiling. Two participants are invited to come forward. Each is given a pen and asked to mark the highest point they can reach on the paper. The trainer than asks them to close their eyes and visualize themselves reaching higher. After a minute, the participants open their eyes and try again. Both are able to reach even higher the second time around. The group applauds the demonstration and the trainer spends the next several minutes discussing the power of positive thinking.

The trainer is passionate about his topic and provides examples—both current and historical—to support his beliefs about the power of visualization and positive thinking. However, despite his considerable enthusiasm, it becomes apparent that the audience's attention has wandered. Can you guess why?

What became of the two people who participated in the demonstration? Both of them were left standing at the front of the room. Since they had not been asked to return to their seats, they remained where they were, wondering whether they would be needed again. As the trainer continued his presentation, they became fidgety and restless. One eventually sat cross-legged on the floor. The audience's reaction finally alerted the trainer that he had forgotten to thank and excuse the volunteers. He paused for a moment and asked the class to give them a round of applause. At this point, he regained the group's attention; however, he had lost a considerable amount of time and learning opportunity while everyone was distracted.

*My thoughts about applying this concept:*

_____

_____

_____

_____

_____

_____

_____

# Key Concept 5

# Contrast

## What It Is

*Contrast* is the brain's tendency to identify certain elements that are different from others in the immediate environment. For example, black letters stand out against a white background. A large red ball is easily distinguishable in a field of green grass. One person standing still in a crowd of moving people is easy to single out. A car alarm sounding off in an otherwise quiet parking lot can be heard at considerable distance. Degrees of contrast depend on the level of differentiation between the elements, with differences based on color, movement, texture, auditory cues, or any variety of sorting variables. As trainers, we can harness the power of contrast to help focus and guide learners' attention, emphasize key concepts, and reinforce recall.

## Why It's Important

During a learning session, participants are bombarded with masses of sensory data. Somehow we need to make the target information (or learning goals) stand out in the learners' minds. We can use contrast to spotlight the central ideas and to increase comprehension and recall. Contrast helps encode key concepts into long-term memory, building a strong foundation to sustain the next stage of learning.

## How to Incorporate It

- In addition to using contrast to highlight single key points *within* a training segment, use it to create a differentiated learning environment on a larger scale. For example, follow a quiet, more focused portion of instruction with a more active session and you will make both sessions stand out in comparison with each other.

- Suppose a brief lecture contains one central idea. Consider having all participants stand and listen for one minute to this important point. Then ask them to *remain* standing while they spend a moment briefly discussing this point with people near them. This change of physical posture will serve to differentiate the piece from the rest of the information. Another option is for participants to stand and discuss this idea *after* you have introduced the point.

- Take the group outside or to another location at a key moment in the session. Once there, teach the primary idea, facilitate a brief discussion, then return to the training room. While the decision to physically relocate the class may seem a somewhat dramatic choice, this drama is the very element that will help participants remember what they have learned.

- Turn the lights down and set a reflective mood when you want participants to relax. This provides contrast for a closing activity or visualization exercise by changing the emotional tone of the room.

- Integrate color, music, humor, and movement to highlight critical information.

## When to Use It

Use contrast whenever you want to emphasize a key point. When you're planning your training, identify the most important information you want to convey and spotlight these learning goals with contrasting moments throughout your training plan.

## When *Not* to Use It

If overused, contrast loses some of its power. This is why it is so important to isolate in advance the most important information and create a plan for emphasizing it. Be sure to use contrast consistently—that is, purposefully. Spotlight *only* the information you deem imperative.

## A Real-Life Training Example

During a session on workplace safety, the trainer found an effective way to maximize the impact of a key point with the use of movement. He presented the point initially in a fast-paced, exuberant way, using plenty of large gestures, a dramatic tone of voice, intense facial expressions, and physical comedy. Finally, when it was clear his point had been made, he stepped into the center of the room and stood completely still for several seconds. While pausing, he made eye contact with the participants and, with a minimum of movement, restated the original point. The contrast between the two styles of presenting, reflected in the trainer's tone of voice and physical gestures, and the pause before speaking, clearly had a dramatic impact. Participants were mesmerized, their attention focused, their recall solidified.

*My thoughts about applying this concept:*

_____

_____

_____

_____

_____

_____

_____

# Key Concept 6

# Precise Directions

## What It Is

Giving *precise directions* is the art of providing clear, sequential, and succinct instructions. It's a unique mode of instruction with a specific purpose—to mobilize learners into some sort of action. Precise directions are useful at each stage of a learning segment—the opening, frame, group activity, debriefing, and closure all require us to give directions. When we transition into direction-giving mode, we need to signal this to participants—perhaps by moving into a different zone (see Key Concept 2) or by shifting our sentence structure and rhythm, tone of voice, or body language.

## Why It's Important

Even in a conventional classroom, teachers need to give directions surprisingly often. In a highly interactive training, we use even more directions. Whether an activity requires only a brief explanation or a whole sequence of steps (outlined on the whiteboard or screen), we can't expect participants to move smoothly and effectively through the learning activity unless they clearly understand their role in each step of the process.

Unclear directions cause a variety of problems. Participants who are unclear about a process may hesitate to involve themselves for fear of doing something wrong. They may quickly wander off task or, worse, think they are on task when they're not. Few trainers enjoy the moment when a participant raises a hand in the middle of a process and utters the dreaded question, "What are we supposed to be doing?"

Moreover, if we give unclear directions too many times (or even once), we put our credibility at stake. It might not be long before learners start thinking: "What else is he going to say that won't make sense? Who is this guy? Could he really be an expert?" Obviously, no trainer wants these thoughts filtering through the minds of participants. The key is to realize before your training even starts just how important it is to provide precise directions in all situations.

## How to Incorporate It

The way we deliver directions should be *congruent* with the message. This means our tone of voice needs to support the primary message and our gestures should aid understanding. Our wording needs to be clear, succinct, and vivid, and we need to stand where we can command the highest level of attention from participants. Each of these elements can add to or detract from participants' understanding.

Here are some tips for making your directions both congruent and clear.

- Be brief, precise, and specific. Practice directions in advance to cut out any unnecessary words. For example, instead of saying, "I want you all to turn to page 42," simply say, "Please turn to page 42." Similarly, instead of saying, "OK now, everybody, what we're going to do is we're going to start by taking out the next case study, which is number 12," simply say, "Please take out case study number 12."

- Give instructions one at a time. Do not bombard participants with multiple instructions. Instead, give them one instruction and allow ample time to complete that task before giving the next instruction. If you have a lengthy sequence of instructions, consider providing them in writing. Otherwise, in the time it takes participants to complete one step of a process, they will forget the next. Each situation is unique, so you will have to look at your material to determine what is best—whether to go step by step, giving one direction at a time, or to provide participants with written information.

- Wait until everyone's attention is focused before giving directions. If participants have just arrived, or are just finishing a task, or they are looking at notes or textbooks, get their full attention first. If necessary, deal with any lingering issues, then again request everyone's full attention before introducing the next task.

- Make your tone of voice and body language *congruent* with the type of directions you are giving. For example, when asking participants to stand up, you might increase the pitch of your voice on the word "up" and raise your arms in an inviting gesture. When asking learners to close their eyes for an activity, you might want to lower your voice, turn down the lights, and perhaps even close your own eyes before speaking.

- Make eye contact with as many (if not all) of your participants as possible as you deliver the directions. Check with the group to ensure they understand the steps involved and the purpose of the activity before starting.

- As described in Key Concept 2, *Bridges and Zones,* make sure you move to the *directional zone* when delivering instructions. This is the area closest to the participants where your proximity helps focus learners' attention and prepare them for action.

- Establish precise time frames when providing directions. For example, if a trainer says, "We'll be moving into groups shortly," participants may immediately begin mentally sorting themselves into groups and miss any subsequent information. They might start wondering, "How long is *shortly?* I'd better hurry; there's not much time get organized! Who do I want (or *not* want) in my group? And what are we going to have to do then?" All this internal dialogue divides and reduces participants' focus. A better approach is to say, "In two minutes, you'll be moving into the same discussion groups you were working with an hour ago." This is a much more precise direction.

- Allow sufficient pauses between each step in the sequence of instructions. To determine whether you're leaving enough time, check in with your audience frequently and regularly, and watch and listen carefully.

- Make the language you use when giving instructions as clear and vivid as possible. For example, instead of saying, "Let's have all the new employees in one group, and everyone else in another group," say, "All the new employees gather together at the back of the room under the clock, and everyone else gather together at the front of the room near the whiteboard." Or, instead of saying, "Turn in your writing assignments" say, "Place your writing assignments on the front table in the wire basket."

## When to Use It

For maximum impact, provide directions and explanations for each step of the process. For example, when preparing learners to take a quiz, instruct them about what supplies they should have in front

of them, where to put their books and other extraneous materials, and what the time expectations are. While providing verbal instructions at every juncture may occasionally appear excessive, it's better to err on the side of clarity than to create chaos. Imprecise directions may confuse, disrupt, and divide participants' attention, ultimately making the training less effective.

## When *Not* to Use It

Giving directions constantly, repeatedly, or indiscriminately—especially *during* activities that demand intense concentration—is likely to distract, disengage, and frustrate participants. It's very tempting to continue to talk or repeat directions after students have begun concentrated work, particularly if you see someone who obviously didn't understand one of the instructions. However, at this point it is much better to check in with those people one-to-one, or answer individual questions quietly, without disturbing the rest of the group.

## A Real-Life Training Example

At one training, I was observing the proceedings from the back of the room when the trainer asked participants to read a specific line from their workbooks. She opened her own book to the appropriate page and said, "Please turn to page 12 and follow along with me." However, as she began to discuss the designated line in the book, I noticed that something wasn't right. While some of the participants had rapidly located the correct page and were following along, many had just found their workbooks, but had yet to find the correct page or line. The rest of the participants *were still looking for their workbooks*. They were busily looking under their chairs, checking their tables, or turning to see whether they had left their workbooks at the back of the room. How much learning do you think was happening at this point? Not much!

A vital step in giving effective directions is to verify that every participant is following along at the appropriate pace. Instead of continuing forward while leaving some members of the audience behind, this trainer could have paused and said, "If you have found page 12, please raise your hand." At this point, she could have carefully looked over the group to verify that everyone was ready to continue.

*My thoughts about applying this concept:*

_____

_____

_____

_____

_____

_____

_____

# Key Concept 7

# Resource Distribution

## What It Is

*Resource distribution* is a simple but smart technique that elevates the otherwise nonproductive downtime required to hand out materials to a higher plane. Instead of leaving participants in an idle holding pattern while we laboriously pass around resources, we can make this time purposeful and productive by providing a little humor, a brief energizer, or a touch of novelty while still achieving the original objective. Such unexpected elements can provide contrast, boost attention, increase motivation, and ultimately enhance comprehension.

## Why It's Important

When the distribution process takes more than thirty seconds, we run the risk of losing learners' attention to restlessness, sedation, or boredom. And once a group's concentration has been lost, it may be difficult to reestablish. Also, since materials are often distributed at the *beginning* of a learning session, this is the very place where we want to engage learners.

## How to Incorporate It

At the very least, request participants' help to distribute resources. Or, better yet, surprise participants by taking a novel, funny, or energizing approach to the task. Here are some ideas to get you started.

- Ask a few participants to help you distribute the materials. Position them at different places in the room and tell the remaining participants they must go "earn" their materials by paying one of these people a compliment.

- Distribute handouts (two alike to each learner) to half of the room. Then ask these learners to stand and deliver their extra handout to a learner on the opposite side. Give them a specific period of time (i.e., thirty seconds) to introduce themselves to each other before returning to their seats. Next time, reverse sides and have learners select someone new to introduce themselves to.

- If you plan to review and/or discuss a handout immediately after distributing it, organize the material in four or five separate stacks and place them in various parts of the room. Divide participants into groups and ask each group to choose a stack, read the handout, and discuss its content. Then reconvene for a large-group discussion.

- Ask participants to move tables to the periphery and then arrange the chairs in a circle in the center of the room. Pass out materials and ask for volunteers to read aloud before following up with a group discussion.

- Arrive early and place resource packets around the training room so they are only slightly visible (i.e., under a table, behind a curtain, or beneath a ledge). When it's time to distribute them, announce that the course materials are hidden in strategic places around the room. Hold one up so participants know what they look like, and tell them that when you say "go," they'll have one minute to find a workbook for themselves and to make sure everyone around them has one as well.

- Put on some high-energy music and ask participants to get up and take a handout from each of the stacks you have set up at the front of the room prior to the session. At the end of the "assembly line," have a stapler or binder available.

All these strategies get learners moving, interacting, and using their brains while also accomplishing the mundane task of distributing resources.

## When to Use It

Distributing materials can be an effective way to incorporate a productive state change. Integrate distribution needs with a stretch break, a surprise, or another energizing activity whenever time allows.

## When *Not* to Use It

If you plan to distribute materials immediately following a fast-paced, energetic learning activity, consider taking a more conventional approach. Rather than energizing the group in this case, you'll want to give them time to catch their breath, relax a moment, and transition into the next learning segment.

---

### A Real-Life Training Example

It was the first day of a training. Participants had arrived and taken their seats. The trainer had introduced herself, and was prepared to get the session under way. She picked up a stack of papers and faced the audience. Holding them up so everyone could see them, she said, "Here is the schedule for this training—the syllabus." She then approached the first row of participants and was about to pass them out when she paused. She announced, "Actually, if you're really interested in what's going to happen, it's up to you to get a syllabus!" With that, she threw the stack of papers high in the air, scattering them everywhere. The stunned participants stared at her for a moment, then quickly moved to pick up one of the papers strewn about.

Why did she behave in this bizarre way? Was it merely a random act of strangeness? Was she close to suffering a nervous breakdown? Or was there a larger purpose behind her actions? In fact, when preparing for this course, this trainer had decided to let the participants know right from the start that not only were they going to have to take some responsibility for their own learning, but the training would be unusual. She could simply have said that, but she knew this surprise tactic would have more impact.

In this instance, the trainer realized that distributing the syllabus represented an opportunity to do something ordinary or a chance to do something *extra*ordinary. The participants were startled into being fully awake, and she could now build on the energy generated by this creative jump start to her training.

*My thoughts about applying this concept:*

_____

_____

_____

_____

_____

_____

_____

# Key Concept 8

# Teach It Standing

## What It Is

*Teaching it standing* is a technique that boosts comprehension by getting participants out of their seats and onto their feet. Traditional learning environments have somehow become erroneously linked to *sitting*, when in fact standing or stretching stimulates blood circulation, which in turn enhances learning. Conversely, sitting for extended periods of time has a sedating affect and can become physically uncomfortable—factors that impede concentration. In an interactive learning environment, there are plenty of opportunities to encourage standing rather than sitting. Teachers and trainers stand, so why not learners?

## Why It's Important

Why do so many learners dread the training room? Perhaps one reason is that, based on their previous experiences in trainings, they know they're going to be sitting in a chair for most of the day. Certainly there is a time and place for sitting in the training environment, such as while taking a test or note-taking. However, making learners sit for extended periods will very likely decrease their attention, motivation, and recall.

## How to Incorporate It

- At the start of each training session, facilitate some deep breathing, stretching, and movement exercises to energize and prepare learners. For example, at the start of each session you might have everyone stand, stretch to the right and left, then back and forward. Repeat this several times. End by asking everyone to raise both hands to the ceiling while taking in a deep breath and exhale as they allow their arms to come down. This whole process might only take thirty to forty-five seconds, yet in this short time your participants will wake up and be able to focus more clearly on the next section of the workshop.

- Conduct a "getting to know you" ritual in which participants stand and introduce themselves to two or three other participants.

- Ask participants to get up and form circles for small-group interaction activities.

- Conduct a short demonstration at the front of the room and have learners gather around to watch.

- Break up forty- to sixty-minute segments of seatwork with a brief energizer. For example, invite participants to get up and walk around the periphery of the room with a partner, discussing the content, while you play some fast, upbeat music.

- As discussed in the previous section, ask participants to gather supplies themselves instead of handing them out.

- Create opportunities for "carousel" activities. For example, have participants add their contributions or ideas to sheets of paper hanging on the walls around the training room.

- If possible, provide a space (usually at the back of the room) that is conducive to standing and moving about during the session.

- Use clipboards to allow participants to take notes while standing.

- Conduct a closing activity that gets participants up and out of their chairs. For example, have the group gather in one large circle while offering and inviting individual acknowledgments.

## When to Use It

Invite participants to stand, stretch their limbs, and energize their brains *any time* during your training when you see attention start to wane. Regardless, if appropriate, try to facilitate a standing exercise, activity, or break approximately every thirty minutes.

## When *Not* to Use It

Of course, there needs to be a balance between standing and sitting activities. Some learning activities, such as test-taking, note-taking, essay writing, and extensive reading, are obviously better suited to sitting. However, we need to intersperse these tasks with standing breaks and activities. Make sure participants have the option to sit if they are unable to stand or don't want to participate in the activity. Try to limit standing activities to three to five minutes, as longer periods can be tiring for some and thus counterproductive to learning.

## A Real-Life Training Example

It *seems* like a typical training setting. The participants come into the room and take a seat, prepared to remain there for the duration of the day. The trainer is at the front of the room arranging stacks of papers and workbooks, which the participants anticipate receiving shortly. Instead, as the remaining participants arrive and take their seats, the trainer introduces himself and asks the members of the group to quickly move their chairs to the sides of the room. Bewildered, the participants comply, buzzing questions to one another about why they're doing this and what's coming next. The trainer then asks the participants to stand in a large circle in the center of the room, where each member is asked to introduce him- or herself to the rest of the group. The trainer then thanks the participants and leads them through five minutes of deep breathing and stretching activities. As he concludes this energizing movement, he asks the group to return their chairs to their previous positions and to take a workbook and syllabus from the front of the room before returning to their seats.

In addition to providing an element of surprise, the trainer in this example was able to effectively energize and prepare his participants for a full day of learning. In addition, he created a sense of emotional safety by allowing participants to get to know one another at the start of the training. Thus the trainer was able to accomplish two tasks at once: to stimulate and prepare the minds and bodies of his learners; and to foster a sense of camaraderie and group cohesiveness.

*My thoughts about applying this concept:*

_____

_____

_____

_____

_____

_____

# Key Concept 9

# Participant Inquiry

## What It Is

*Participant inquiry* is a technique whereby the trainer poses carefully worded questions to involve learners early in a training while minimizing emotional risk. Such questions encourage participants to reveal information about themselves and their experience with the subject matter in a way that does not "put them on the spot." As learners are encouraged to share, they feel valued and acknowledged. We need to know who our participants are before we can effectively train them. Participant inquiry not only helps you determine the extent of your learners' knowledge and experience, it facilitates a sense of group cohesiveness as participants discover common ground and open up to each other.

## Why It's Important

Even a *minimal* level of threat can throw the brain into survival mode at the expense of concentration and higher-order thinking. By contrast, a sense of group cohesion can facilitate an immediate sense of safety. The training environment (indeed, *any* new learning situation) can be scary for many people. Unless we dispel this sense of fear quickly and replace it with a sense of commonality, learning can suffer. What is considered threatening varies between individuals; however, when nervous learners realize they will not be embarrassed or ridiculed before the group, and that they are valued and acknowledged for who they are and what they have to contribute, they begin to feel safe. This leaves the brain free to focus on learning.

## How to Incorporate It

- Preface group questions with words and phrases that elicit brief hand responses, yet still acknowledge individual experiences. Here are a few examples:

  Raise your hand if . . . ?
  How many of you . . . ?
  How many of you would like to . . . ?
  How many of you have ever . . . ?
  How many of you are going to one day . . . ?
  How many of you believe that . . . ?

- Prepare a series of questions to ask at the start of your training and at various points during the session. You'll want the questions to be relevant to the learning objectives, as well as to the participants themselves. For example, "Raise your hand if you can already see some ways you can incorporate this idea into you next sales presentation," or, "How many of you have ever faced an awkward moment with a client similar to what I'm describing right now?"

- Design safe questions that invite participants to talk about themselves, their experiences, where they're from, what they want to gain from the training, and why they're there. Questions that are *too* personal or not clearly related can embarrass participants and cause withdrawal—the opposite response from the one you're seeking. For example, a safe question might be, "Share with your group how you came to be working for this company." By contrast, "Describe your most embarrassing moment in a professional situation" might be too personal.

- Think of the *kind* of information you'd like to elicit from learners prior to asking the questions. For example, you might ask, "Does anyone have a personal experience related to this example that might be productive to share with the group? Great, Alex. Can you give us a one-minute synopsis of what happened to you in this situation?"

## When to Use It

We can use participant inquiry throughout a training session; however, it is especially important to initiate early on in a session as trust and rapport are being established. The technique is also effective for

- bringing the audience's focus back when they've been distracted;
- revitalizing a passive group;
- increasing participation;
- shedding greater light or perspective on a topic; and
- determining participants' background or level of exposure to a topic.

You can also use participant responses to transition the group from one topic to the next or to conclude a learning segment.

## When *Not* to Use It

Used too often, participant inquiry can feel contrived and unproductive. So we need to establish a balance between trainer input and participant responses. Remember to set time expectations on how long a participant should speak, and try to tactfully cut short participants who don't know when to stop talking. This can be very disruptive and frustrating for the rest of the group, and erodes the trainer's authority. A good way to curb people who tend to dominate the response time is by mentioning in advance how long you want them to speak, such as saying, "In thirty seconds or less, share with us how you handled that situation," or, "In two or three sentences, please sum up what helped you to succeed in that situation."

Also, be careful not to ask overly engaging questions when time is limited or when you are seeking a specific response. And be aware that, if participant inquiry is not purposeful and skillfully guided, it can diffuse participants' focus, rather than sharpening it.

---

### A Real-Life Training Example

The trainer welcomed participants to the beginning of a weekend workshop. She introduced herself, made a few brief opening remarks, then asked the following series of questions:

"I'm interested in knowing where some of you traveled from to be here today. Please raise your hand if you're from the local area."

[Some participants raised their hands.]

"Thank you. Now please raise your hand if you're from within the state of California."

[More participants raised their hands.]

"Great, now, how many of you have traveled from somewhere outside the state of California?

"It's nice to know that we have people here from so many different places. Whether you're from near or far, thank you for your efforts in getting here today. Let's give everyone a hand."

In the above example, the trainer immediately shows interest in her learners. Participants begin to relax and warm to each other as they find common ground. And, most important, they unconsciously begin to trust that their trainer cares about them as individuals.

*My thoughts about applying this concept:*

---

---

---

---

---

---

---

# Key Concept 10

# Adequate Response Time

## What It Is

The human brain needs *adequate response time* to shift gears between different mental tasks such as listening and verbalizing. Although the brain operates very rapidly, occasionally during a presentation it must make a distinct shift in how it is processing information, and these shifts do not happen instantaneously. For example, moving from listening to a lecture to responding to questions is a distinct change from one task to another. In this case, first the brain must shift from a passive listening state to one that is conducive to active participation. Second, it must process the new information in relation to the question posed. Third, it must generate the appropriate words necessary for verbally expressing the response. And, finally, it must deal with the emotional aspects of offering an opinion in public. Simply put, *this process takes time!*

So how much time should we give participants to go through this process when soliciting a response from the group? Clearly, this will vary from individual to individual and be influenced by the complexity of the information and the learner's prior knowledge. However, a good rule of thumb is to consistently lean toward providing too much (versus too little) time for learners to shift their thinking. If you apply this concept consistently, you'll notice an increase in the quality of responses, as well as a wider diversity of respondents.

## Why It's Important

The downside of asking for responses too quickly is that it may encourage participants with extremely efficient mental processes and/or prior knowledge of the subject to dominate the interaction. Once this pattern is established, it is difficult to undo and has potentially dangerous consequences. For example, participants who take more time to process a response may come to believe they aren't as sharp as their peers, despite the fact that they may be making more connections and thinking more critically than the faster responders. Perhaps worse, if they know they are unlikely to have a chance to share their ideas, they won't even bother to think about the question. Thus, if we allow the verbally quick participants to dominate discussions, we may unwittingly create a counterproductive cycle. Moreover, since the thinking process itself is vital to meaningful learning and long-term recall, we need to encourage it!

## How to Incorporate It

Whenever you ask participants to shift mental gears in the course of a training session, give them sufficient time to mentally prepare. Here are some suggestions for helping your participants transition smoothly from one thinking task to another.

- Before asking for questions at the end of a lecture, invite participants to spend one minute talking to each other about their reactions to the concept being presented. Then ask them to see whether anyone has a specific question concerning the material. Finally, have them thank their partners, face to face, and present their questions.

- Break up a lengthy lecture or other passive presentation by asking participants to turn to the person next to them and summarize what they've heard or learned in the previous ten minutes. Give them a specific time frame within which to conclude the exercise.

- Give participants two to three minutes to write down anything they want about a topic—thoughts, questions, concerns, or insights—before facilitating a group discussion.

- Prepare several different types of questions to elicit supportive responses. For example, if the phrase, "Any comments or questions?" does not elicit a response, have some more pointed and specific questions prepared. Here are a few examples:

- Which parts of this concept need to be clarified?
- How might you apply this principle in your own life?
- How does this lesson relate to the concept we discussed earlier?
- Has anyone used this concept before to solve a problem? If so, how?
- How many of you agree that . . . ? How many disagree? Why or why not?

## When to Use It

The more complex the learning and the less exposure participants have to a topic, the more mental processing time they need. Try to break up large chunks of learning time with activities that require a mental shift of focus. For example, after a lecture invite partner interactions or small-group discussions. Or facilitate a question-and-answer time before asking learners to write about a topic. Or break up independent learning activities with group discussions. And when you want participants to transition back to listening mode, remember to give them adequate time for that as well. A good way to ensure that everyone is ready to move ahead is to ask for a physical signal, such as, "If you feel like you have a fairly good handle on this concept, and are ready to begin the next section, please give me a thumbs up."

## When *Not* to Use It

*Adequate time* is a relative term. If *most* participants are ready to respond quickly, less wait time would be appropriate. The key is reading your audience accurately—not just those in the front row or those closest to you, but those at the back of the room as well. If you notice that a wide variety of learners are volunteering responses and you like the quality of the responses you're getting, you're likely providing adequate time. If, however, the responses don't meet your expectations, try extending the response time.

---

### A Real-Life Training Example

At the end of a fifteen-minute presentation, a trainer says the classic words, "Any questions?" When this overly used and trite request is answered with the classic blank group stare, she quickly returns to lecturing. At the end of the next segment, she repeats the line, "Now, are there any questions?" She waits a few seconds, looks up at the clock and continues, "Come on, people! Weren't you listening? Don't you care? This is important material! You *must* pay attention!"

By handling the situation in this way, the trainer is not creating a positive atmosphere for learning. Even if someone is brave enough at this point to tentatively pose a question, the situation is strained. This result is not what the trainer hoped for, and her chance to generate a lively discussion has passed.

How would you have handled the situation?

The trainer should have realized that the learners' blank stares were quite possibly *external* expressions of a complex *internal* process occurring within the brain. Had she done so, she might have had the patience to guide them through the mental shift necessary to process the information, prepare a response, and articulate their questions.

*My thoughts about applying this concept:*

_____

_____

_____

_____

_____

_____

_____

# Key Concept 11

# Specify Response Mode

## What It Is

*Specifying response mode*—or stating *how* you want questions answered—is a useful strategy for establishing a sense of certainty among learners, which is a fundamental precursor to facilitating a lively group discussion. Put simply, if we merely ask, "Are you ready to begin?" we might not get much of a response. However, we're much more likely to get a higher level of response when we are very specific about how we expect learners to respond, such as saying, "*Raise your hand* if you're ready to begin."

## Why It's Important

While there are many reasons why participants fail to speak up in a group setting, occasionally it's because they are uncertain about *how* we expect them to respond. When our brain is concerned with *how* to respond to an inquiry, our verbal responses may be more hesitant. This is because, when uncertainties sift through our unconscious mind, higher-order thinking and verbal communication functions end up taking a back seat to the more immediate concerns of status and appearance.

Participants left to play a guessing game in the training room will digress to basic human operating principles—that is, *no* response is safer than the *wrong* response. In other words, if we leave participants to judge what's *right* or *wrong* about *how* they respond, which means facing the possibility of *looking bad,* many of them would rather not respond to a trainer's question.

By contrast, when we clearly communicate our expectations, we create a more relaxed environment in which learners feel safe, secure, and certain about what we expect of them, and are therefore more likely to respond. Once we've established a basic level of trust, participants are more likely to involve themselves in the discussion.

## How to Incorporate It

Questions that include a specific direction for how to respond, such as those listed below, help shift learners into the appropriate response mode and increase participation. You should be able to rephrase most questions to specify a response appropriate to your specific context, audience, and topic. In the following comparison, the questions on the left omit the response mode, while the alternative on the right includes it.

| *No Specific Response* | *Imperative* |
| --- | --- |
| Is everyone ready to begin? | Smile if you're ready to begin. |
| Have you got the right page? | Nod if you're on page 16. |
| Did you have a good lunch? | If you had a good lunch, stand up and stretch. |
| Does this make sense? | If this concept makes sense, give me a thumbs-up. |
| Who's finished? | If you're finished, look up toward the front of the room. |
| Does everyone have the handout? | If you've received your handout, hold it up in the air. |
| Are there any questions? | If you have a question, please raise your hand. |

For the best results, phrase your questions using positive language and consistently incorporate physical gestures that support the request. For example, asking, "Who doesn't understand?" does not indicate what physical response is being asked for, and also focuses on the *negative* side of the question. It would be more appropriate to ask, "Raise your hand if you feel as if you have a fairly good grasp of this concept." Focusing on the positive means participants will feel more comfortable about responding. However, it still provides you with the information you need to know—if some participants do *not* raise their hands, perhaps you could get most people involved in an activity while focusing on assisting these people privately to gain a better understanding of the material so everyone can move forward to the next step in the process.

## When to Use It

Specifying the response mode is particularly important in the early stages of a training session when you are establishing a basic level of trust in the room. Providing clear expectations right from the start helps foster a sense of safety and supportive risk-taking. Later— perhaps when the "crest of the wave" has arrived—one way of changing the state of the participants might be to ask questions where the specified response mode is something novel, such as asking participants to "Stand up if . . . " or "Point one elbow at the ceiling if . . . " or "Wiggle your pen in the air if . . . "

This technique is also helpful for warming up breakout groups, mixing up modes of participant involvement, involving participants quickly and efficiently, and transitioning from one learning task to another—such as when moving a group from viewing a video to discussing it.

## When *Not* to Use It

It may not be necessary to continue specifying the desired response after you establish expectations and/or they become inherent.

For example, once you've embedded the pattern of raising hands, you don't need to provide additional prompting unless you wish to shift learners to another mode. However, if you do shift to a different expected response, you'll need to repeat it several times until everyone knows what is now expected of them when a question is asked.

Be sure to specify a response mode that is suitable for the type of participant you're training. For example, specifying a response mode that carries the potential of embarrassing some individuals (such as asking a group of police officers to sit on the floor) could be counterproductive. The role of the trainer, in most circumstances, is to *increase* the level of comfort and trust in a group.

---

### A Real-Life Training Example

Participants in a technical writing seminar were at the tail end of a thirty-minute writing exercise. The trainer wanted to conclude the exercise and initiate group discussions. He asked participants to spend the next two minutes completing the assignment.

The trainer proceeded to busy himself with paperwork, then looked up and said, "Is everyone ready to get into groups?" No one responded, and he noticed that a few participants were still bent over their papers. Immediately recognizing his mistake, he rephrased the question and the response was immediate.

"We'll begin group discussions in thirty seconds, so please finish up your writing at this time." After waiting until every one had put down their pens, he said, "Thank you, move your chairs into a small circle and wait for the next set of instructions."

What happened? Initially, the trainer failed to anticipate what kind of transition would be necessary to move learners from a high-concentration task with an internal focus to one that required an external focus and an inherent understanding of the trainer's response expectation. Some learners were so involved they didn't even hear the question. When, however, the trainer realized what was happening, he was able to rephrase the question and include clear expectations. Thus he eliminated the guessing game and replaced paralysis with purpose.

*My thoughts about applying this concept:*

_____

_____

_____

_____

_____

_____

_____

# Key Concept 12

# Question/Clarify/ Question

## What It Is

The *question/clarify/question* sequence increases meaningful group dialogue by *priming* participants' brains properly for this task. It consists of the following three distinct components:

1. Ask the discussion **question** to provide an *overall perspective.*

2. Provide **clarify**ing *details* or examples to model the type of response you're looking for.

3. *Repeat* the original **question** or instruction to serve as a launching point for the discussion.

Each element in the formula plays an important role in priming the brain for higher-order thinking, lively dialogue, and a clear and productive group focus.

## Why It's Important

Engaging a group in lively and productive discussion is a valuable tool for teaching adult learners. However, this is easier said than done—especially when some participants are introverts, nervous, or perhaps even overawed by more senior members of the group. Even with an extrovert, confident group, if we aren't clear about what we want to achieve or we fail to engage participants and keep them focused, the discussion can lose valuable momentum.

To create a productive discussion we need to make sure participants have a

- basic understanding of the *topic* to be discussed so they can start thinking about it for a few moments in advance of the discussion actually beginning;

- precise understanding of the trainer's line of *thinking* about the topic so their discussion can more closely adhere to the intended focus; and

- *reminder* of the original question so discussion does not fixate on the most recent detail or example the trainer has provided.

If participants are not clearly informed about any of these three factors, the discussion can easily turn unproductive. Thus, using the question/clarify/question format can set the stage for a stimulating, successful, and focused discussion.

## How to Incorporate It

- State the original question cleanly and carefully, making certain the central point of the upcoming discussion is clear to everyone.

- In the second section, use only three or four examples. Too many details at this point may confuse the original issue. And, when choosing *which* clarifying examples or details to include, make them as distinct from each other as possible. For example, suppose the original question is, "Discuss how this strategy might be useful to you." The clarifying examples might be, "How could this be used with you team at work?", "How might it be helpful when dealing with your boss?", and "Might it even be an idea you could share with your family?"

- To initiate a successful discussion, repeat the original question and *say nothing more!* Anything further added here will most likely confuse the situation. End cleanly by repeating the original question and then simply say, "Begin."

- Using language in this manner requires precision. Before you incorporate this technique into your trainings, plan and practice exactly what you are going to use for each of the three steps. Explore several ways you could do it and then, in the actual training, present the most thorough, yet most precise, version you can generate.

## When to Use It

In general, follow the question/clarify/question format whenever you are setting up a group discussion. Although the technique can be used effectively at any time during a training, it is especially helpful in the early stages of a session when trainers are seeking to establish a relationship of trust and safety within a group. Carefully applying the strategy early on sets the tone for productive discussions. This foundation of having had successful group interactions is particularly useful later in the session if topics become more complex or challenging.

## When *Not* to Use It

You don't have to use this technique with instructions that are very short and explicit. For example, if you are using the prior key concept, *specify response mode,* with a simple instruction such as, "When you're done writing, please put down your pen or pencil," no further elaboration is needed. If you can make your point clearly in one sentence, do it!

---

### A Real-Life Training Example

It was during a workshop for staff trainers at a large corporation that I first realized the need for this technique. Ironically, I was conducting a segment on *how to give effective instructions* when I made the connection.

My training plan involved facilitating several brief activities with an involved set of directions. After the group completed the activities, I asked them to break into small groups to discuss what they had noticed about the way I had provided the initial instructions. Each group noted comments on a sheet of paper and then chose a spokesperson to read them to the whole group.

The purpose of the follow-up discussion was to increase awareness about the *specifics* of giving effective instructions, such as word choice, length, structure, vocal tonality, and the use of supporting body language. While a few of the comments were related to the specifics I had in mind, most were vague and nonproductive, such as, "Your instructions were very good and clear." Since an answer like this does little to move the conversation forward, valuable time was wasted as I tried to gently weed out the misguided comments. Finally, I narrowed the

*(Continued)*

(Continued)

responses down to those that were instructive, but had I been more clear about what I wanted learners to focus on, the exercise would have been much more productive.

Later, I thought about the experience and considered how I might stimulate a more dynamic discussion next time. I decided I would share the objective of my questioning with the group, rather than expect them to read my mind. I also realized that I'd been encountering this hurdle at several other points in my workshops.

At that point, I began to use the question/clarify/question format as a way to organize my thoughts to ensure completeness. In the very next workshop, I initiated the same group discussion using this technique:

1. "As trainers I'm sure you all understand the importance of clear and specific directions. When participants understand what you expect of them, your lessons have significantly greater impact. As groups, please use my own instruction delivery as a case study, and consider what aspects of it impacted your understanding, clarity, and follow through."

2. "For example, what did you notice about the words I chose, the tone of my voice, or the gestures I used in leading the activities we have done in this workshop?"

3. "Please discuss in your group what aspects of my instruction impacted your understanding, clarity, and follow through."

This approach—offering a rationale coupled with specific expectations and a reiteration of the initial instruction—has since produced significantly better results.

*My thoughts about applying this concept:*

_____

_____

_____

_____

_____

_____

_____

# Key Concept 13

# Managing Disruptions

## What It Is

Disruptive behavior is an unwelcome guest at the training table. Regardless of age, stage, or setting, there will occasionally be those who seek attention at the expense of others. And yet there's a fine line between seeking attention and contributing. The key, therefore, is to recognize and find a productive way to handle these attention seekers before they have the chance to upstage the trainer. Most of the time these individuals are natural-born leaders whose energy, if channeled properly, can enhance rather than disrupt a training session.

One technique for *managing disruptions* is to provide a sanctioned forum whereby participants can share the spotlight for a time. Interestingly, when attention seekers are recognized and legitimized, the problem usually dissipates. By integrating time for participant humor, sharing, and leadership into your training plan, you not only put an official "stamp of approval" on *appropriate* ways to receive attention, you reduce the problem of *inappropriate* responses that divide and disrupt a group.

## Why It's Important

Disruptions test our credibility as trainers because, for at least a moment, we lose control of the room. The way we handle such moments determines both how quickly we regain control and whether we go up or down in the group's estimation. So, even when remarks are relatively harmless, we need to manage disruptive participants by being firm yet diplomatic, and taking back control as quickly as possible.

TrainSmart trainers maintain control of a group with a subtle but strong guiding hand. The most effective way to accomplish this is to provide a forum for attention-seeking learners in a trainer-controlled activity that reinforces positive humor, leadership, and participation. This will provide an outlet for the people who would otherwise seek attention by hijacking your agenda.

Perhaps the most debilitating form of disruption is *sarcasm*— a Greek word meaning to "tear out the flesh with the teeth." While good-natured joking and harmless humor can enhance group cohesiveness, sarcasm can alienate participants very quickly. Rather than ignoring sarcastic comments, consider how you might bring these inappropriately vocal constituents into the fold. People who are "quick-witted" are often quite intelligent and, if guided correctly, have the potential to make a powerful and positive contribution. Humor that does not rely on stereotypes or poke fun at others can help focus attention, build group cohesion, increase recall, break down resistance, and reduce stress. And it can add an element of joy to an otherwise routine learning task or topic.

## How to Incorporate It

Here are some ideas for channeling disruptions and fostering humor in the training environment.

- Right from the start of any training, share with participants how the day/session will proceed, what your expectations are, and how they can actively contribute. Knowing immediately that they will have plenty of chances to participate may lessen the need of some people to seek attention at the start of a training.

- Provide time early on in the training for participants to share something about themselves and/or an opportunity for them to get acquainted with one other and you. Sometimes being the center of attention within a small-group context is enough for some potentially disruptive participants.

- Disruptions may be a signal that it is time to move on to the next activity. The first time a participant exhibits potentially disruptive behavior, you may wish to ignore it. However, if it continues, immediately initiate an activity. For example, you might transition into small-group discussions if it is appropriate, or facilitate a quick energizer.

- Provide a "funny-bone forum" in which participants have the opportunity to share a joke or funny observation with the rest of the group. Provide a set of ground rules before initiating this activity (i.e., no disparaging remarks or jokes that rely on stereotyping).

- Give groups an opportunity to perform content-related skits or role plays. Ensure that individuals who like the limelight have an appropriate outlet to showcase their abilities.

- Give participants an opportunity to voice any concerns or objections. Sometimes just providing time to "clear the air" can offset potential problems.

- Avoid preaching to or engaging with an argumentative participant. If the remark is relatively harmless, just say, "You might be right," or, "I see your point," and move on. Simply acknowledging individuals rather than allowing them to upset you keeps the focus on the training and the task at hand.

- Project self-assurance with relaxed but focused body language. Have a plan but remain flexible so that extenuating circumstances can be accommodated with ease. Remain calm and self-possessed when interacting with attention seekers. The goal is to maintain control of the group climate, *not* necessarily individuals.

- Use peer pressure to diffuse inappropriate behaviors. For example, if a participant continues to be a problem after you've tried other techniques to productively channel his or her energy, defer to the group. Say, for example, "What do the rest of you think about John's position or opinion on this?" Or ask them, "If you were a trainer and had to handle a heckler, how would you do it?" At the very least, this technique gives you time to strategize your next step.

- *Always* confront remarks that hurt others, regardless of *who* made them or *why, when,* and *how* they were made. Deal with these individuals firmly and directly. Ask them to refrain from other offensive remarks in your presence and during the training. If they do not comply, you may have to ask them to leave.

## When to Use It

Although some behaviors or comments may not distract you, they may be distracting to participants. Therefore, it is best *not* to ignore them. There are appropriate times to use subtle techniques to diffuse disruptive behavior and appropriate times to use more direct ones. When making this judgment call, consider the situation and the persistence of the problem. For example, if a participant has been disruptive on several occasions, and none of the more subtle strategies you've tried have worked, perhaps it's time to take a break and speak privately with that person about the issue and the behavior you expect in the training room.

Channeling disruptions into appropriate forms and forums is an ongoing process that begins in the early planning stages of a training and continues throughout. Once you have established a respectful and credible command of the group, disruptions usually cease to be a problem. Just remember that some personalities are compelled to be in the limelight, so respond with appropriate opportunities for everyone to shine.

## When *Not* to Use It

Do not discourage light-hearted, good-natured humor. There is no better way to break up the tension of an intense learning environment than with a good laugh. Be careful not to be too controlling or overly sensitive; occasionally, even poking fun at yourself can be an extremely effective way to earn respect. In fact, it's not a bad idea to keep a few jokes up your own sleeve for moments that call for humor. If someone's remarks are cutting or hurtful, don't use subtle channeling strategies. Instead, ask the person directly and firmly to cease making the remarks. If that person can't comply, ask him or her to leave.

---

### A Real-Life Training Example

Early on in a staff development workshop, a trainer realized she had a few sarcastic males in the group and their remarks were getting slightly out of hand. At the earliest opportunity, she asked the audience to form small groups and discuss the following question: "What do you think are the most common causes of lost productivity in the workplace?" She asked the groups to record their top five reasons. And she added, "Here's the catch: at least one of these reasons *must be sarcastic or funny!*"

As they went to work generating responses, one could hear bursts of laughter erupting from various areas of the room, and there was a palpable rise in energy. When it came time to give their responses, the trainer asked that they share only the *humorous* ones. When the comedic interlude reached a crescendo, and the participants began to wind down, the trainer said, "Those were great. Thanks. Now, on a more serious note, what other causes of lost productivity did you identify?"

The group could sense a clear shift in expectations. The trainer indirectly, although quite clearly, channeled the sarcasm into an appropriate activity while also setting some parameters to limit its use. The strategy worked: the trainer supported some good-natured humor while also making the group *explicitly* aware that more joking at this point would be inappropriate.

*My thoughts about applying this concept:*

_____

_____

_____

_____

_____

_____

_____

# Key Concept 14

# Creative Note-Taking

## What It Is

Absorbing, analyzing, and storing new information in the brain is a complex enterprise—one that is greatly aided by the process of transferring information to paper. Most people recognize that *note-taking* is one way to reinforce memory, and many of us depend on this learning tool. But did you know that *creative note-taking*— sometimes referred to as mind mapping—further enhances comprehension and recall?

Mind mapping is a process where learners depict major themes and concepts from the learning with colorful symbols, images, notations, and connecting lines that represent relationships. Creative note-taking optimizes learning and recall because it moves us through the process of analyzing information (left-brain function) with a creative emphasis (right-brain function), thus encouraging connections across brain hemispheres.

## Why It's Important

Traditional note-taking, where we try to write down everything we hear, can put the brain into "scramble mode." The more hectic this state becomes, and the longer it is sustained, the less time we have to process and thus retain the information. However, when participants discover more creative and effective note-taking techniques, the brain relaxes and learning increases!

Mind maps are made up of the images, ideas, or stories that give context and meaning to the trainer's words. Words are much easier to remember when associated with symbols, colors, and concrete images. *Drawing notes* in the fashion of mind mapping frees up the brain to pursue other higher-level cognitive functions, such as linking new learning to prior knowledge, recognizing patterns, and critically analyzing information from various perspectives.

## How to Incorporate It

Give learners a brief overview of the mind-mapping process. Show them a few examples of mind maps or other creative note-taking techniques before starting your presentation.

- Supply the appropriate materials: *color* markers or pencils and oversize paper. Consider taking participants through a brief mind-mapping process to clear up any confusion.
- Pause often when delivering content. Every fifteen minutes, provide a few moments for learners to review their notes and ask questions. During this time, encourage participants to add lines, words, or symbols to their mind maps to clarify and organize their thinking.
- Create your own mind map, depicting the key concepts related to your presentation and share it with learners early on in the presentation and/or at the conclusion. This provides a valuable overview or road map of the ground you expect to cover, then summarizes it again when you close.
- Encourage participants to share their mind maps with each other. The more they discuss their interpretations, the deeper the material will be encoded in their memory. Incorporate small-group mind mapping in which the emphasis is on teamwork, or have individuals discuss their respective mind maps in small groups.
- Hang participants' mind maps around the room and have everyone walk around and view them.

## When to Use It

Make time for creative note-taking whenever you present new content. Nurture the process by allowing participants adequate time to record the material. And introduce them to techniques, such as mind mapping, that encourage crossovers between right and left brain hemispheres. Encourage participants to review and clarify material with you and each other during brief but regular breaks.

## When *Not* to Use It

Discourage participants from taking notes during activities that involve their active participation or discussion. If you are about to shift from a note-taking mode to one that's more conducive to verbal participation, help participants make the transition by facilitating an informal interaction with a neighbor, a brief break, or a quick movement activity.

---

### A Real-Life Training Example

The setting was a four-day personal and professional development seminar facilitated extensively throughout the United States, Asia, New Zealand, and Australia. Right from the start, the trainer delivered the content with an unusual pattern of speech. He would pause just before the last word of a sentence and wait for participants to complete it (in their minds, if not out loud). For example, he might say, "Hopefully it's now clear what I've been trying to . . . *explain*." He would not actually say the word *explain* until someone in the audience had said it. If no one responded out loud, he would sometimes just continue with the next sentence, never completing the last.

It was a curious approach to content delivery. In a conversation during a break, someone asked the presenter why he did it. He explained that the technique encouraged participants to stay more involved in the learning process. From a theoretical perspective, the idea made some sense. From a personal perspective, however, I confess that I found it mildly irritating— although not enough to significantly impact my experience in general.

Early on the third day, however, I witnessed an occasion where the approach definitely did *not* work. The trainer had been lecturing about a topic that was of considerable interest to the group: how to make lots of money! At one point, he presented an idea that especially captured the attention of participants. Everyone was furiously scribbling in their workbooks.

At that exact moment, the trainer paused at the end of a sentence—waiting, as usual, for the audience to fill in the blank. This time, however, no one responded. When his pause was greeted with silence, he glared intensely at the audience and said, "Come on, people! You can do better than this! This is important information, and the only way you're going to get it is to stay awake!"

Strong words, yet I was chuckling inside. As a trainer, he had made a serious miscalculation. He'd failed to recognize *why* people had not responded: they were actively engaged in note-taking! In this case, the trainer *interfered* with the learning process by disengaging participants, rather than engaging them.

Since the trainer wanted to facilitate interaction, it would have been better to either discourage note-taking or allow a transition time for participants to mentally shift gears. A thirty-second pause to allow them to complete their notes would have made a dramatic difference to the audience's response.

*My thoughts about applying this concept:*

_____

_____

_____

_____

_____

_____

_____

# Key Concept 15

# Positive Language

## What It Is

*Positive language* maximizes the chances of participants' understanding and responding positively to a request by making it in *positive* terms. Consider how *you* feel when somebody *tells* you what to do rather than *suggesting* a plan. For example, how do you think you might react internally to the directive, "I want you to introduce yourself to the people sitting next to you"? Compare this with the request, "Let's take a few minutes to introduce ourselves to the people around us." Most adult learners would prefer the second form—especially as the relationship of mutual trust and respect is being established.

A person's most likely internal response to overly aggressive command language—although it is often unconscious—is to resist the trainer's directions regardless of their potential value. Positive language, on the other hand, can open up learning as quickly as aggressive language can shut it down. If you want to empower participants while increasing productive training time, get into the habit of communicating requests in a cooperative fashion using positive terms and diplomatic language.

## Why It's Important

When our words trigger a negative response in participants, they lose critical concentration and focus. Conversely, when we use positive and cooperative language, it engenders a sense of sincerity, trust, and a willingness to follow our lead—all essential factors for successful trainings. Creating a positive environment leaves the participant's mind free to focus on what's truly important: the learning at hand.

## How to Incorporate It

Carefully crafted language is a powerful vehicle for helping participants to achieve learning objectives. Here are some examples.

| Language Choices That Might Trigger a Negative Response | Positive Language Alternatives to Create a More Positive, Cooperative Feeling |
|---|---|
| 1. "I want you to find your group and sit down with them." | "Please find your group and sit down with them, and we'll be able to get started promptly." |
| 2. "Raise your hand if you've lived in this state for only two years or less." | "If you have lived in this state for more than two years, please raise your hand." |
| 3. "I need all of the teenagers to form a group there, while you adults gather over here." | "Those of you slightly under twenty, please join me in this group, while those of you slightly over twenty join the group near the door." |

### Commentary

In example 1, the phrase "*I want you to*" implies a relationship of dominance or power over participants. When we use dominant communication patterns with participants, we tend to elicit internal resistance—if not external rebellion. In the alternative positive language, the simple word *please* motivates participants to respond. By being courteous, we prime them (subconsciously) to respond positively to our request.

In example 2, the word *only* has a negative connotation. Simply altering the request by dropping the word only, or rephrasing it in positive terms, makes a world of difference.

In example 3, the word *teenagers* is sometimes construed as a negative label, so if we use it to distinguish or set apart the group, younger participants may feel insecure, if not threatened. For the older group, just as many teenagers would rather be adults, many adults would prefer to be much younger! The use of the word *slightly,* accompanied by a tone of gentle humor in the trainer's voice, should achieve the same result with significantly less potential resistance.

## When to Use It

Given the objective is to turn learners *on*, not *off*, there are few times when it *doesn't* pay to craft our language throughout a session more sensitively. However, it is especially important to consciously use positive language when using a word to which some participants may be sensitive.

When first working with a new group, we need to be as diplomatic and gentle as possible. While it may seem overwhelming to do this consistently, once you experience the positive and productive difference it makes in your training environment, you'll embed positive language into every interaction. Eventually it will become a valuable addition to your training tool kit.

## When *Not* to Use It

With the exception of a few hard-core training environments such as boot camp or military school, it is *always* a good idea to use positive and inclusive terms such as *we, let's,* and *our,* rather than preachy, dominant directives like *You should, I want you to,* or *You need to.* The only time a command using these words is more productive is in the event of an emergency or potentially dangerous situation. If, for example, an unexplained fire alarm sounds, a command like, "Leave your things and file out the back door immediately!" is perfectly appropriate.

---

### A Real-Life Training Example

A visiting principal is organizing a room full of school teachers for breakout discussions. He decides that spreading the newer teachers out among the groups will facilitate the most productive discussions. Thus he inquires with a smile, "How many of you here are just rookies?"

The principal is quite surprised when his slightly sarcastic comment is not received with much enthusiasm. Rather, he experiences a number of silent stares and mildly hostile facial expressions. Some of the participants even look downright mad. After a few seconds, a bold participant raises her hand and remarks, "How do you define 'rookie'? I've been a teacher for only three years, but I certainly don't feel like a rookie!" The principal realizes his mistake, apologizes, and eventually rephrases his request with more diplomacy. "Please raise your hand if you've just recently begun bringing your talents to the field of education."

In this case, why should the principal single out participants for lack of experience when he has the perfect opportunity to recognize the value they will bring to many students for years to come? The principal's second attempt made many more participants shine with pride, and he avoided making them feel inadequate or under-recognized.

*My thoughts about applying this concept:*

_____

_____

_____

_____

_____

_____

# Key Concept 16

# Involve, Don't Tell

## What It Is

The concept of *involve, don't tell* moves away from the traditional education model that simply tells participants, "This is what you need to know, now repeat (memorize) it." Transmitting information in this way sacrifices involvement on a deeper level and doesn't allow participants any personal processing time. However, when we encourage participants to analyze concepts and make connections *through their own mental efforts*, their recall increases significantly.

## Why It's Important

When people are actively involved in the learning process, they encode the information along multiple memory pathways—physical, mental, and emotional—which embeds it more deeply into their long-term memory. Active involvement can also increase heart and respiratory rates, thus raising mental and physical energy. Participants who have journeyed actively through a learning process, rather than just being on the receiving end of it, walk away from the session with more than just a hazy cerebral sense of a topic: they take a physical—and likely emotional—memory with them. This establishes a solid foundation of meaning and enthusiasm on which we can build the next level of learning.

## How to Incorporate It

- Pause regularly and *ask* participants *what they think* the key points are. If the responses you're aiming for aren't provided, facilitate a process of deduction by posing additional pointed questions to guide the group's thinking.

- At various intervals during a presentation, organize participants into small groups to complete a relevant task or exercise, and then regroup for a debriefing.

- Occasionally stop and ask participants to write down their thoughts and/or questions and address these issues as soon as possible.

- When feasible, give participants the opportunity to learn through experimentation. Applying new learning increases comprehension and recall.

- Performing role plays, skits, and other theatrical games and creative activities taps into the right cerebral hemisphere—the area of our brain that synthesizes information.

- If you want to ensure recall, "get physical." For example, second-language teachers have discovered that students learn foreign vocabulary better when new words are attached to a consistent movement. Thus, rather than standing at the front of the room and telling students that the way to say *jump* in Spanish is *"brinca,"* the TrainSmart educator would ask the group to stand and jump in place while shouting *"brinca."*

## When to Use It

Try to involve participants as much as possible *throughout* a training. While lectures have a place in the training environment, other modes of learning with frequent active involvement will be more successful at reaching the full spectrum of learning styles. Involvement is especially important when participants have minimal background and/or experience in the subject or skill set. And, because openings and closings are critical junctures in the training process, you can be especially influential by actively involving participants at these times.

## When Not to Use It

There is a fine line between presenting *too much* information and *not enough*. Learners clearly need *some* content to put the new learning into context. For example, you certainly can't expect learners to engage in a productive discussion about a subject they know very little about. The key is to find an effective balance between content delivery and active learning.

---

### A Real-Life Training Example

Arizona's Junior Miss was touring her home state giving a series of brief presentations. The topic of her speech was "Domestic Violence in the State of Arizona." During her talk, she threw a question out to the audience: "Did you know that last year 35% of women who visited Arizona emergency rooms were there as a result of domestic violence?"

Her goal in posing the question was to emphasize and reinforce the most important point of her presentation—the depth of the problem and the lack of awareness about it. But did her delivery maximize the potential *impact* of this important message? She shared a shockingly high statistic—at least, it was shocking to me. Yet some of its force was lost because the speaker *told* the audience, instead of choosing to involve them in discovering it.

Later, we brainstormed different ideas for presenting this key fact in a way that would engage the audience more meaningfully and actively. This is the one she chose:

At the next presentation, she asked all participants to raise their hand. Then she posed the following question sequence: "What percentage of women do you think visit Arizona emergency rooms as a result of domestic violence each year? If you think it's 5 percent, go ahead and put your hand down. If you think it's 10 percent, put your hand down." She continued along this line of questioning, increasing the statistic in 5-percent increments. By the time she reached 25 percent, most of the audience had lowered their hands. When she announced that the number was even higher, the effect was dramatic. By involving the audience physically and mentally in the learning process, she increased the likelihood of their recalling this statistic.

*My thoughts about applying this concept:*

_____

_____

_____

_____

_____

_____

_____

# Key Concept 17

# Ownership

## What It Is

*Ownership* refers to the value participants derive from being included in decision-making processes during a training. When participants feel their own voice matters, a subtle yet important shift in perspective and energy occurs. They move from being a *passive receiver* to an *active explorer.*

When participants are given the opportunity to be involved at the decision-making level, *they no longer sit back and expect the trainer to train them: they become stakeholders in their own success.* This group dynamic not only produces a more stimulating training environment, it balances the onus of responsibility between the trainer and participants.

## Why It's Important

Nothing drives progress faster than vesting everyone in the process. Commerce has capitalized on this concept for many years: some of the most profitable businesses are employee-owned corporations or companies that offer stock options or profit-sharing incentives.

In a training, when participants feel empowered they tend to accept more responsibility for the conditions around them. This shift in perception makes them more receptive, and it improves cognition and recall. This is because ownership gives learning *meaning*, which plays a critical role in cognition.

## How to Incorporate It

To create ownership, we must begin with an attitude of deep respect for others' experiences and for the collaborative process itself. This means emphasizing, *in both words and actions,* that everyone plays an important role in the training process. Here are just a few of the ways you can foster collaboration and show how much you value everyone's contribution.

- Ask the group to create their own list of ground rules at the start of the training.
- Let participants alter seating arrangements as they see fit for the particular exercise or task at hand. For example, rather than saying, "Group A will meet at the back of the room," ask the group to determine *where they would like to meet.* Provide location boundaries if necessary.
- Rather than defining a set of terms for participants, provide a "fill in the blanks" worksheet that offers clues—perhaps like a crossword puzzle. Ask participants to meet in small groups or teams to complete the exercise, then regroup for a debriefing and answer-sharing session.
- Invite teams or individuals (depending on time constraints) to facilitate a portion of the training. It could be as simple as leading a two-minute stretch break or as involved as asking teams to plan and facilitate a complete lesson.
- At the beginning of a session, share a schedule outline with participants and ask them whether it seems reasonable. Ask them whether the break and lunch times are sufficient, whether the learning goals are clear, and whether they have any questions or concerns. Take into account their issues and, if possible, adjust the schedule to reflect their needs.
- Frequently solicit others' viewpoints. If time is a factor (it almost always is), break into small groups so more people have the opportunity to be heard.
- Near the end of the training, give participants the opportunity to share their perspectives on what was effective and what wasn't. Perhaps use a brief evaluation or feedback form.

## When to Use It

Establish a sense of ownership *early on,* and then consistently and appropriately *reinforce it throughout the training.* Once you have empowered participants with a sense of ownership, you'll need to continue providing opportunities for them to experience it. While there may be some decisions that are not negotiable or appropriate for class involvement, *most* aspects of a training session are or can be.

For example, you might allow participants to decide *how* they will be evaluated. You can prevent this from eating into training time by providing a narrow list of choices and facilitating a quick vote.

## When *Not* to Use It

Of course, we can't involve participants in *all* the decisions. In fact, this would practically guarantee a less than optimal training. We have to make many decisions about content, delivery, and the setting itself long before the day of the training. So determine in advance *what aspects* of the training are *appropriate* for participant involvement, and include participants whenever possible.

---

### A Real-Life Training Example

A trainer walks to the front of the room. She smiles and says, "Good morning, my name is Cristal. As we begin, I thought it might be appropriate for us to take a few minutes to get acquainted with each other. First I'd like to answer any questions you may have about my background. Perhaps, you're wondering what qualifies me to facilitate this training today, or maybe you want to know why I do what I do or for how long I've been doing it. I've found this process works best if you write down your questions on the index card in your packet. Please take one minute to do this. When you're done, place your card here on the table. I'll address as many of your questions as I can in a ten-minute period."

Rather than telling the audience about herself, the trainer has effectively involved the participants in the first process of the workshop. They now have a vested interest in what happens right at the start of the day. She has provided very specific instructions, in a tone that is inclusive and cooperative.

*My thoughts about applying this concept:*

_____

_____

_____

_____

_____

_____

_____

# Key Concept 18

# Pause
# for Visuals

## What It Is

*Pausing for visuals* (e.g., PowerPoint slides, flip-charts, handouts) reflects the brain's need for time to free itself from competing stimuli before it can organize incoming visual data. The more novel or complex the visual data, the more time the brain needs to organize it.

## Why It's Important

Pausing for visuals avoids forcing participants to divide their attention between two competing stimuli. When competing stimuli split learners' attention, they tend to tune out. The learning brain can't possibly pay *full* attention to both elements at once, so it shuts down one or both sensory streams.

For example, have you ever been in a situation in which somebody attempts to explain something to you while you're trying to read about it? The experience is frustrating at best, and at worst stops your learning. We can avoid this learning impediment by allowing participants' brains a moment of quiet contemplation to process new visual information before we tell them about it.

This not only increases learning enjoyment, it improves participants' comprehension and recall.

## How to Incorporate It

If you are in the habit of talking as soon as you click on the next slide, pausing for visuals may initially prove a little challenging. One way of working around the habit is to explain a concept *before* you bring up the slide. Since many people are primarily visual learners, however, it is usually best to let participants study the slide in silence for a minute or two. While you pause, breathe deeply and think "SWAE (Show, Wait, Ask, Explain)." This approach may feel awkward at first, but soon it will become automatic. The following tips can support this process.

- Once learners have had a moment to process the new information, *ask* them what they think they do and don't understand. They may surprise you with some very relevant questions. Not only will you have encouraged them to use their brain, you will have actively *involved* them in the learning process (see Key Concept 16: Involve, Don't Tell).

- Provide *additional* processing time if you're not providing a copy of your PowerPoint presentation, since many learners feel compelled to take notes or diagram them.

- When appropriate, supply participants with a copy of your PowerPoint slides with the training notes so they can review them while waiting for the session to begin.

- Post flip-chart pages on the walls around the training room so participants can review them during breaks or between activities.

- Before you talk about new visual material, ask learners to discuss it in pairs or small groups.

- Avoid Death by PowerPoint: give participants plenty of regular and frequent pauses to allow them sufficient time to process the material. Also, try not to rely on PowerPoint to drive the entire training session.

- Remember that when using PowerPoint or overheads, lights will often have to be dimmed, and this may make some people sleepy. Avoid leaving the lights lowered for more than ten minutes.

- In general, people can process only a limited number of visuals— perhaps ten to fifteen—before their effectiveness diminishes. To increase participant recall, use visuals only as needed, and be sure to keep participation as interactive as possible.

- One way to maintain interest when using visuals might be to occasionally add some variety in terms of the *type* of visuals being shown, such as adding in photographs or cartoons, or anything that might bring some novelty into the presentation.

# PAUSE FOR VISUALS

- How long to pause between visuals is a judgment that you'll have to make moment by moment, depending on factors such as the complexity of information, learners' experience with or background knowledge of the subject, and the apparent degree of understanding displayed by participants.

## When to Use It

Make a habit of *always* pausing for visuals. The length of time will vary, but you should apply the practice consistently.

## When *Not* to Use It

A *long* pause may not be necessary when visuals are *reviewing* a topic or when you're displaying uncomplicated images such as photographs. However, even these circumstances warrant a brief pause to allow the brain to reorient itself and register the image.

## A Real-Life Training Example

A corporate trainer presents a series of very impressive PowerPoint images intended to familiarize department heads with a new business model the company is eager to implement. The managers furiously scribble notes while the trainer flips from one slide to the next, supplementing the images with thoughtful explanations.

The presentation is flawless, except for one thing. The trainer is completely oblivious to the fact that participants are falling farther and farther behind. When he finally stops talking long enough to observe the audience, he notices that quite a few people look confused. He realizes they may have some questions. He solicits them, but only one manager responds. Her question clearly illustrates that she didn't process the information on the slides.

This experience reminds the trainer how important it is to provide intermittent pauses between visuals. He decides that, at the very next training, he will tape a postcard with the acronym SWAE on his computer stand to remind him to Show, Wait, Ask, and then Explain!

*My thoughts about applying this concept:*

_____

_____

_____

_____

_____

_____

# Key Concept 19

# Press
# and Release

## What It Is

*Press and release* reflects the natural ebb and flow between participants' ability to concentrate and their need to relax and mentally refresh themselves. While *press* represents the intense focus required for participants to acquire new information, *release* represents the subsequent "letting go" period that both supports participants in consolidating the new material and diffuses their mental and physical tension.

## Why It's Important

Although *some* individuals may be able to sustain longer periods of deep concentration, continuous mental effort is generally *not good* for learning.

If we don't carefully balance concentrated study with time to relax and consolidate the learning, participants may feel frustrated or bored. Eventually, they may even become exhausted or feel like failures for not being able to grasp the material. Such feelings, especially when occurring regularly, can hinder learning.

Without regular *release*, participants are likely to feel stressed and strained, and may fall off task by daydreaming or "spacing out." Worse, they may simply choose not to come back to future sessions. Conversely, when trainings are well-balanced between press and release activities, participants not only rate sessions more enthusiastically, they comprehend and remember more.

## How to Incorporate It

- The more complex or novel the material, the more frequently you'll want to incorporate release activities.

- During lengthy press periods, introduce intermittent opportunities for release. For example, ask participants to turn to a neighbor and briefly share what they've gleaned so far from the lesson. Provide guiding questions to keep it simple, quick, and relevant. Perhaps follow up with a large-group discussion and address any lingering questions, concerns, or comments.

- Mediums such as journal writing, small-group discussion, role-playing, mind mapping, games, or art are useful for both releasing and debriefing after new learning.

- Encourage release within work groups by inviting them to include debriefing periods in their team meetings. Suggest a simple question-and-comment period, an acknowledgment activity, or a team ritual.

- Give participants who are learning in a language other than their native tongue extra release activities to balance the additional learning effort. You could also relieve the pressure by offering opportunities to discuss the new learning *in the participant's first language* if possible.

- Provide regular, brief, unstructured breaks.

- Use energizers or other movement activities to introduce or debrief new learning.

- Prepare a variety of physical energizers to throw in if the wave crests before you were expecting it to. Even simple techniques such as asking participants to stand or turn their chairs to face a new direction can serve to reenergize the group.

- In a free-form learning environment such as group activities, mature learners tend to create their own releases. If participants seem to temporarily fall off topic, don't be too quick to push them back into the group—they may need a moment of release and will rejoin the group with renewed focus after a minute or two.

- Visualization or brainstorming exercises generally constitute a *press* activity as participants concentrate and focus inward. After such exercises, provide a *release* by encouraging participants to share their experience in writing or in a small-group discussion format.

## When to Use It

Introduce a release activity of some kind before any learning session that requires focused concentration. As a general rule for adult learners, break up press periods every twenty minutes with a release activity; however, if you're presenting in a lecture format, if the material is unusually complex or novel, or if participants aren't learning in their native language, provide additional opportunities for release.

## When *Not* to Use It

Think of press and release as a mutually inclusive dynamic that works like a teeter-totter. It is natural for one end of the teeter-totter to rise while the other falls, but a shift in weight is necessary to restore balance. However, *temporary* imbalances are not necessarily bad: they can induce moderate levels of stress, which actually drive learning and augment retention.

---

### A Real-Life Training Example

Participants were about to start the first phase of an activity challenging them to solve a difficult problem. Although they were organized into small groups, the trainer asked them to consider the problem independently first in silence for two minutes before beginning the group-work phase of the exercise. "When I start the music, please consider it a signal to refocus your thoughts here in the room and chat quietly with your group while you wait for my next set of instructions," he explained.

After two minutes, the trainer began playing a selection from a Mozart CD and continued writing a series of questions on the chalkboard. While participants waited for their next set of instructions, an air of mystery filled the room and they began talking to each other. Assuming the trainer understood the concept of press and release, what do you think he intended to accomplish during this unexplained pocket of time?

In this case, he had enough experience to know that if he did not allow individuals the opportunity to debrief with each other for a few minutes, their attention in the large-group discussion would be greatly reduced. Talking informally was the release

---

the trainer knew participants would need after a few minutes of concentrated effort. Thus he wisely chose to encourage a period of informal exchange, effectively preparing participants for the next phase of the exercise.

*My thoughts about applying this concept:*

_____

_____

_____

_____

_____

_____

_____

# Key Concept 20

# Purposeful Body Language

## What It Is

Our body talks, and often it speaks louder than our words! Do you know what yours is saying? Our body language can either reinforce the information we are presenting or distract participants and interfere with their learning process. *Purposeful body language* means supporting content delivery by aligning it with integrated verbal and physical cues. Training smart means communicating on multiple levels to deliver a well-integrated, believable message.

## Why It's Important

Body language is critical in the training environment because the brain registers visual cues such as facial expressions, body movement, eye contact, and hand gestures on a subconscious level. While we read body language unconsciously in a training, we can consciously use our body language to help communicate critical ideas, and focus participants' attention in a given direction.

## How to Incorporate It

A trainer's body language, when orchestrated purposefully, can help to maintain learners' attention, facilitate a particular pace, highlight important points, enhance recall, and build trust. It is critical, however, that it be done in a natural, relaxed manner. Here are some ideas to help you align your verbal and physical communication styles.

- Watch a videotape recording of yourself and identify which gestures you feel support your message and which (if any) negate your message or are not in alignment with what you are communicating. Also, if possible, watch a video of a public figure you admire and respect. Almost all effective speakers reinforce their verbal ideas through their body language.

- Practice your presentation in front of a mirror, and experiment with various supportive gestures and facial expressions. Determine which key points you want to emphasize and incorporate a specific technique for achieving this effect at these junctures.

- Adjust the *magnitude* of your gestures to reflect the *level* of emphasis you want to achieve. For example, when you deliver the *most* important facts in your presentation, use large body movements, dramatic gestures, and direct eye contact.

- Complete stillness can also grab learners' attention and highlight an important point, especially when it is in contrast to your usual movements. Pause for a few seconds, make direct eye contact with the audience, tell them you are about to reveal a key piece of information, and *then* make the point.

- Consider your position/location in the room and your posture relative to the type of atmosphere you wish to create. These cues represent significant aspects of communication. If, for example, you're facilitating an intimate activity such as a poetry reading, sit *among* participants on their level rather than stand over them. If you want participants to listen carefully, stand up front and walk back and forth as appropriate. Pause occasionally to emphasize key concepts.

- Rather than holding your fingers up to indicate a first, second, and third element, use broader, more obvious gestures such as the following to clearly distinguish one element from the next: (1) first hold both hands clearly to the left of your body to represent the first element; (2) then hold your hands in front of your body to emphasize the second element; and (3) then hold your hands clearly to the right side of your body while introducing the third element. Alternatively, you could move to three different places in the front of the room while introducing the elements.

- When moving from one subject to another, visually demonstrate the transition by shifting your body movements or your position in the room (see Key Concept 2: Bridges and Zones).

## When to Use It

While it may be impossible to be completely aware of every nuance in your body language all the time, it is quite possible to purposefully incorporate gestures that support your verbal message most of the time. This is the goal of using purposeful body language.

## When *Not* to Use It

Not every word, phrase, or sentence requires an accompanying gesture or movement. In fact, they can easily be overdone. In addition, not every gesture needs to be carefully calculated and precisely timed. Rather, your goal should be to develop a natural style in front of the room, which is contrasted by moments where the body language highlights and adds emphasis to certain key moments in the presentation.

---

### A Real-Life Training Example

A trainer was addressing the three most important principles of effective communication. She told the participants a story about a manager who had successfully employed these principles in the workplace. While explaining the example, she sat casually on the edge of her desk and assumed a very relaxed posture and conversational tone.

At the end of the story, she stood up, walked over to the whiteboard, picked up a marking pen, and in a slightly louder voice said, "Please raise your hand if you recognize any of the communication techniques I've just demonstrated. Let's discuss the impact they made." The responses came fast and furious. The audience's attention was definitely focused. From the quality of responses she received, the trainer knew that, in fact, the most important parts of her presentation had been clearly demonstrated.

---

*My thoughts about applying this concept:*

_____

_____

_____

_____

_____

_____

_____

_____

# Key Concept 21

# Visual-Field Variations

## What It Is

The *visual field* is a person's entire view from a particular vantage point. In the seminar setting, a participant's visual field is the trainer's "stage." The concept of *visual-field variations* reflects the idea that we need to use this stage to its full potential. How many seminars have you attended, for example, where the walls are bare, there are neat rows of chairs, and a simple podium or table is at the front of the room—all of which remain unchanged throughout the session? Maximizing the visual field means attending to the *total* training environment, including walls, bulletin boards, ceilings and windows, using props, displays, images, and posters. When we use our *entire* teaching stage, our training becomes akin to a surround-sound experience, advancing learning to a new level.

We can vary the visual field by repositioning ourselves, repositioning participants, or modifying the room.

Take another look at your training room.

- Are the walls and display areas full of colorful and relevant images and information?
- Are the visual aids attractive and easy to read from a distance?
- Is the room full of interesting objects, models, and manipulatives?
- How often do they change relative to the content presented?
- How frequently can participants shift their seat or position in the room?

## Why It's Important

Using the full spectrum of a learner's visual field and changing it often create higher levels of concentration and recall. Shifts in the visual field wake up the brain and keep learners alert. Because participants naturally shift their range of vision from the presenter to others around them, to close-up material, to surrounding displays, we need to make sure that what they see supports the learning. If they see interesting, relevant, and novel images around them, their concentration is more likely to remain focused on the learning at hand. Support materials of this type can positively impact a participant's *implicit memory*—a mental process whereby information and images are registered in the brain and encoded without conscious effort.

## How to Incorporate It

### Planning

Incorporate visual-field changes into your training plan using the ideas below. Plan to *change* participants' view often and create or assemble a set of visual materials you will use to support each teaching segment.

### Preparing

When preparing a training room, walk around and view it from multiple perspectives to make sure your displays and support materials attend to participants' entire visual field. Be sure your posters or images use color as much as possible. If the information you are covering allows for it, use a variety of *types* of images, from humorous ones to graphs, charts, and photographs.

### Training

Here are just a few ideas to help you vary the visual field during your training.

- Participants tend to sit in the same location in a room once they've established it as "theirs." This makes them comfortable; however, it can eventually lead to a feeling of stagnation or detachment in a training session. To keep the setting fresh and participants mentally alert, occasionally suggest participants change their position in the room. Explain the value of doing this and tell them they are welcome to find a new seat or move their chair any time they begin to feel bored or distracted.

- Use activities that require various room arrangements. For example, ask participants to move their chairs into a circle for a group discussion. "Circle time" can help break the ice in a new group or support a check-in or get-acquainted activity. Consider what participants see while sitting in rows of chairs versus a circle. How does viewing others' faces versus the back of their heads potentially impact learning?

- Periodically change the direction from which you are presenting. For example, ask participants to stand and turn their chairs 180 degrees toward what has so far been the "back" of the room. This unexpected request, coupled with the physical effort it entails and the shift in visual field, stimulates anticipation and renews focus. If you are using flip-charts, consider having one already set up at the back of the room to make this shift as easy as possible.

- Place visuals in *every* area of the room so when participants' attention inevitably shifts, they see material *relevant* to the presentation. Hang items from the ceiling, on the door, and on the windows. Pay special attention to bulletin boards and display areas. Provide visually stimulating handouts and make them very accessible.

- If using PowerPoint, remember to include "holding" slides to support the times in a training when you're not directly referring to the screen. For example, for breaks include a slide that reminds participants when they're expected back or, if you're moving into an interactive activity, use a cartoon or photograph to introduce and act as a backdrop to the event.

- Post the flip-charts created through small- or large-group discussions around the room.

- In a multiple-day training, post photographs on a bulletin board of participants engaged in learning activities from a previous session.

- Provide opportunities for participants to present to the rest of the group from different parts of the room.

- If possible, occasionally use the outdoor spaces surrounding the training area. Going outside briefly creates a novel variation in the visual field and refreshes the brain.

## When to Use It

Plan on implementing visual-field shifts throughout the training session. However, in case you need to refresh the group more often, have a host of visual-field variation strategies at your fingertips to use when you sense the need. Regardless of how interesting or compelling you are as a trainer, learners do inevitably look away. The TrainSmart presenter understands this dynamic and is well prepared for it.

## When *Not* to Use It

It is sometimes a good idea to *suggest* rather than *direct* participants to make a visual field shift. And there are times—such as while testing—when a shift would not be appropriate. The goal, of course, is to support, not disrupt, the learning process.

---

### A Real-Life Training Example

A staff-development trainer was well into the third day of a four-day training when she noticed a lower-than-usual energy level in the room. A number of people looked glassy-eyed and others seemed distracted. She also noted that most participants had continued to sit each day in the same chair. The seating was typical—rows of chairs facing the front of the room.

The trainer decided a visual field shift might help restore learners' attention, so she offered the following: "Let's take a few minutes to stand, stretch, and breathe." After leading a few deep-breathing and stretching exercises, the trainer added, "Great. Now, everyone please move your chair into the center of the room in a large U shape with the top of the U open to the chalkboard."

As the participants rearranged their chairs, the trainer noticed a significant energy shift. Participants were talking to each other, and their faces looked more animated. Once the chairs were moved, the trainer positioned the flip-chart at the top of the U. Every person now had a clear view of the presenter, the visual aids, and each other. As she resumed her presentation, the trainer noted she had reclaimed the group's focus.

---

*My thoughts about applying this concept:*

_____

_____

_____

_____

_____

_____

# Key Concept 22

# Vocal Italics

## What It Is

*Vocal italics* is the art of supporting new learning by

- *providing time* for participants to comprehend new terms;
- *emphasizing* new terms with a change in volume and/or vocal tone; and
- *repeating* new terms verbally several times if needed.

When we introduce unfamiliar concepts or technical terms, vocal italics give participants the additional time they need to process and understand these new ideas.

## Why It's Important

A trainer's primary goal is simple: we want participants to remember the material we present. Otherwise, why teach it? For learners to understand new concepts and remember them, they need to internalize unfamiliar terms. Accommodating and supporting this process is critical to comprehension. By using vocal italics, we alert participants' brains to listen more carefully, thus supporting the learning process.

## How to Incorporate It

- In the planning stage of your presentation, highlight potentially unfamiliar terms and concepts.

- During the training, punctuate new terms with pauses and vocal shifts. For example, the following fact might be italicized in this way: "When government hunters in Africa *cull* a herd of elephants, they kill certain members to ultimately benefit the herd. *Culling* is a resource-management practice whereby the size of the herd is balanced with the available *geographic resources.*" In this example, the trainer pauses just before and after the italicized words, clearly stresses the pronunciation, and then repeats terms for further emphasis. Here's another example: "This is known as *oxidation. Oxidation* is the process by which *oxygen* causes some metals to form rust."

- In addition to using vocal italics, monitor your audience carefully for signs of confusion or frustration. If you notice vacant, puzzled, or anxious facial expressions, slow down, repeat new terms and concepts, and facilitate a partner-share or question-and-answer period to ensure all participants understand the new terminology.

## When to Use It

This concept is most critical when the content you're presenting is unfamiliar to your participants. The more prior knowledge your participants have regarding the subject, the faster you can present. If you have a mixed group, aim your delivery toward the middle of the experience range, rather than toward the top or bottom. Ask yourself how familiar the *average* participant is with this content. Then proceed accordingly, always adjusting as you go. If participants seem confused, slow down, vocally punctuate new terms and concepts, use terms repeatedly, and then check in with your audience again.

## When *Not* to Use It

Don't use vocal italics to subject matter experts, as it may appear patronizing. In general, however, you can use this technique to aid comprehension when explaining any concept you believe will be unfamiliar to the average participant.

---

### A Real-Life Training Example

A large manufacturing firm held a training session on electrical safety for all of its employees. The trainer was an electrical

*(Continued)*

---

(Continued)

engineer with a graduate degree and many years of experience in the field.

During the presentation, he used terms such as *amperes, watts,* and *volts.* Although he provided a brief definition of these and other industry-related words, his delivery was rapid. Some of the employees, many of them nonprofessional-level staff, were familiar with the terms, but others had little reason to use them.

Eventually, one dismayed participant raised her hand and said, "Could you please slow down and explain some of the terms you're using? I'm a little confused."

Several other participants nodded their heads in agreement, alerting the trainer that he'd lost much of his audience. Good-naturedly, he apologized to the group and recapped what he'd presented. This time he slowed down, paused frequently, used vocal inflection, and repeated unfamiliar terms in a variety of contexts. Before proceeding, he facilitated an exercise in which small groups were asked to brainstorm common workplace safety dangers and precautions. During the exercise, he walked around and answered individuals' questions.

The trainer's initial inclination—to direct the training to the highest common denominator (i.e., those participants most experienced with the content)—was clearly off base. However, when he altered his course and employed vocal italics, the trainer reclaimed his audience.

*My thoughts about applying this concept:*

_____

_____

_____

_____

_____

_____

# Key Concept 23

# Music Matters

## What It Is

The fact that music can facilitate a state change in our mind/body makes it a potentially powerful tool for trainers. Not only can *music,* when it is used purposefully, help reduce stress, it can enhance cognition, memory, and emotional intelligence. We also know that music can induce relaxation, creativity, self-discipline, and motivation.

## Why It's Important

Since music has an immediate physical, emotional, and psychological effect on human beings, it can help build social connections, heighten awareness, and provide a sense of safety. It floods the brain in rhythms and beats that induce a wide range of states from energized to relaxed. What better way is there to tap into the emotions and consciousness of a learner than with the music they love?

As trainers, we can tap into music's ability to enrich the training environment. At the very least, music can enhance motivation, attention, and feelings of vigor. Beyond this, research in recent years has suggested it may also improve various brain functions such as spatial-temporal reasoning skills. Other studies suggest that music listening can increase levels of norepinephrine and epinephrine—two neurotransmitters linked to emotional arousal—in the brain. While particular music rhythms may stimulate the right hemisphere of the brain (creative thinking, synthesis), other rhythms tend to predominately stimulate the left hemisphere (analytical thinking). Still other researchers note that music's memory- and image-evoking ability stems from its tendency to overlap the auditory cortex with the part of the visual cortex that deals with visual association. Although this body of science is still young, there's very little downside to playing music—so give it a try!

## How to Incorporate It

Here are a few easy ways to integrate music into your trainings.

- Play an up-tempo selection to energize a group or set a lively mood.
- Play a slow-tempo selection to calm a group or set an inspirational mood.
- Play nature-inspired music or a Baroque selection to focus participants or to set a mood for concentrated study.
- Play music during transitional activities—for example, while participants pick up handouts or reorganize their chairs.
- Use a particular song to call a group back from a break or cue participants that the next part of the session is about to begin—much like the theater does when intermission is over.
- When choosing a stereo system, consider the parameters of your particular training milieu (i.e., volume requirements, training room acoustics, remote-control feature, load capacity, and ease of use).
- Individual preferences regarding music type and volume always vary. Either direct your choices toward the norm or play a variety of selections at varying levels to accommodate the widest range of listeners.
- CDs are certainly a convenient medium for music in the training environment. However, if you have access to a digital music player—for example, an iPod—you will have even greater control over your music. Digital music players allow you to store an incredibly large number of songs, so you'll have more to choose from than if you just brought a stack of CDs. You can usually find a particular song very rapidly. You can also easily create playlists—a sequence of songs you've chosen to use for a particular module of your training. These are just a few of the many additional aspects of music that a digital music player will allow you to explore.

# MUSIC IS THE UNIVERSAL LANGUAGE.

## When to Use It

- *Before a training session begins* (while waiting for participants to arrive), play mood-setting music to encourage friendly exchange among learners. A quiet room can be intimidating and impersonal. Music at the start of a session can also set a positive tone for the rest of the training. In addition, it provides the opportunity for a clear, nonverbal starting point when it's time to begin: simply turn the music off to seize the moment *without* having to say, "Okay, it's time to stop talking and direct your attention toward me."

- *During transitions or break activities,* energize a group with an upbeat tune.

- *During small-group discussions,* soft background music without lyrics can "pad" conversations and reduce distractions.

- *Close a session* with an inspirational tune that carries a memorable message. Participants will walk away from the training with this as their last impression.

## When *Not* to Use It

Don't play music, even softly, during testing or content-heavy presentation periods that require intense concentration. At such times, it is best not to introduce any competing stimuli.

---

### A Real-Life Training Example

In a large one-day workshop for school administrators, participants were divided into two groups. Group A was instructed to meet in the Amber Room, while Group B was directed to meet in the Blue Room. After a logistical briefing, participants were told to take a five-minute break before joining their respective breakout sessions.

The two seminar rooms were set up exactly the same, except that the Amber Room contained a portable stereo playing upbeat tunes moderately loud. As the group filed in from their break, music sent a wave of positive energy through the room.

The Blue Room, however, had no music, so when participants entered all that could be heard was a dull hum generated by a couple of participants talking quietly among themselves.

The trainer in the Amber Room incorporated music throughout the breakout session, while the Blue Room's trainer did not. Otherwise, the same curriculum was addressed in the two sessions. Two participants in each group were asked to be silent observers—to sit back, observe, and take notes on the group dynamics and degree of involvement.

Participants in the Amber Room bounced in and immediately began talking to others in the room. The trainer used music on and off throughout the session. Participants in the Blue Room, on the other hand, shuffled in and sat down quietly. No music was incorporated.

Afterward, participants were asked to return to the general session, where they were debriefed on the structural differences between the two breakout sessions. The participant observers were asked to share their notes and then the larger group was asked to share its impressions. The differences were striking. Participants in the Amber Room clearly got more out of the session than those in the Blue Room.

---

*My thoughts about applying this concept:*

_____

_____

_____

_____

_____

_____

_____

_____

# Key Concept 24

# Guiding Attention

## What It Is

*Guiding attention* is the technique of facilitating smooth transitions from one learning task to the next by *inviting learners with verbal and/ or nonverbal cues to shift their focus gradually* toward the next activity. Guiding attention helps stop participants from tuning out and *recaptures* learners' attention after small-group exercises, breaks, and/ or independent-learning periods.

## Why It's Important

Guiding attention ensures the brain has sufficient time to transition from one learning activity to the next. Guiding attention is particularly important in a highly interactive environment where the training plan calls for frequent shifts—for example, from a lecture presentation to a dyad interaction to a small-group activity, and so on. While a range of learning modes is highly beneficial to learning, if we don't manage these frequent transitions carefully, they may disrupt the flow of the workshop.

For example, after an activity such as an independent learning task or break, we can regain learners' attention by emphasizing meaningful relationships between learning activities.

## How to Incorporate It

The following techniques are just a few of the ways to gain, maintain, and/or regain participants' attention during transition periods.

- When giving instructions for an upcoming learning activity, include a precise time frame and wrap-up cue. For example, you might say, "At five minutes to three o'clock, I'll announce that you have five more minutes. Please start wrapping up your small-group discussions at that time. At three o'clock, we'll regroup to discuss your conclusions." Note that a precise time frame was provided as well as a specific cue—the announcement—for initiating the transition.

- Make requests instead of demands. A directive such as, "Okay, everybody, stop talking and look up here now" is jarring and lacks sensitivity to a participant's own learning process. Rather, prepare the group ahead of time, and then ask a question or make a request that is germane to the assignment. For example, you might say, "Over the next thirty seconds, as you bring your group discussion to a close, please consider what three elements you personally feel are most important to managing a successful learning organization."

- To regain a group's attention, initially use a voice that is *slightly* louder than the noise level in the room. Then immediately lower your voice so participants have to pay attention to hear you. The key is to synchronize the momentary break in noise level with a reduction in your own volume.

- Always give participants a heads up a few minutes before they need to conclude their present activity. This gives the brain time to prepare for the necessary mental shift. When you use music to alert participants, you avoid having to raise your voice and/or the possibility of being perceived as overbearing.

- If you need to unexpectedly gain participants' attention, consider standing on something to make you higher than they are. Moving a chair to the middle of the room and standing up on it is one option. Raise your hand above your head and ask participants for their attention. Wait patiently while conversations are wrapped up. As soon as the room is quiet, put your hand down and make your announcement.

- Rather than making an abrupt shift to a new topic, bridge the old with the new. For example, you could invite participants to share what insights they gleaned from the activity being wrapped up and then briefly relate their responses to the upcoming activity.

## When to Use It

Try to incorporate guiding strategies right from the start of a training session. If you use this strategy at the very beginning, participants will come to expect it as a natural part of the rhythm of your presentation style. If you handle these early transitions clearly and cleanly in the opening moments, the group will naturally be inclined to follow this pattern for the rest of the training. Continue to use these strategies as consistently as possible whenever a transition is needed.

## When *Not* to Use It

Try not to rush closure, especially if the group's energy level is high and participants are deeply involved. While we can't give every activity extra time, try to remain flexible throughout a training and don't pack too much content into any one learning session.

---

### A Real-Life Training Example

Participants in a workshop were divided into small groups for a brainstorming activity. They were told they had thirty minutes to complete the exercise, and they would be alerted halfway into the allotted time period. Fifteen minutes into the activity, the trainer was pleased to see that most of the participants were fully engaged in an animated discussion and rapidly jotting down notes.

A few minutes later, a very faint, almost imperceptible level of classical music could be heard. About five minutes later, the music became a bit louder, at which point the participants realized they were nearing the closing time. The trainer steadily increased the volume over the next five minutes as discussions wound down. Finally, the trainer lowered the volume slightly and said, "Please take the next minute to wrap up. Let's reconvene at five after the hour to discuss your responses."

By steadily increasing the volume of the music, while keeping it appropriate at all times, the trainer allows participants to experience a smooth transition to the next activity.

---

*My thoughts about applying this concept:*

_____

_____

_____

_____

_____

_____

_____

# Key Concept 25

# Verbal Specificity

## What It Is

*Verbal specificity* maximizes comprehension by communicating accurate details with precise, positive language. This type of explicit detail helps the brain translate content into concrete, easy-to-grasp images that paint an accurate and intentional picture in the mind's eye. For example, the word *not* can conjure up the very image one wants to avoid. If we say to our participants, "Do *not* imagine a huge pink gorilla," what actually happens , of course, is exactly the opposite of our intent. Thus we can see the importance of using positive and precise language in the training environment.

## Why It's Important

Since new learning is often accompanied by feelings of frustration and/or stress, anything we can do to reduce confusion and improve communication is beneficial. For example, imagine you are going bird watching for the first time. The binoculars you have are old and don't stay focused, so you get frustrated and give up. How do you feel about bird watching? You think it's annoying and not very rewarding. Now imagine your first bird-watching trip was with an experienced guide who brought along first-rate equipment and quickly helped you learn to spot and identify birds. This time you enjoyed the experience, remembered it in detail, and wanted to repeat it. When we're learning something new, clarity and understanding both keep us on task and reduce frustration and/or confusion.

Verbal specificity is also important when we're giving instructions, as demonstrated in the following example.

Midway through a CPR certification course, the instructor distributes a handout that summarizes the key points discussed so far. He asks participants to spend the next five minutes reviewing the handout to prepare for the certification test later in the day. He provides the following instructions:

"As you review this handout, pay particular attention to the case studies on page two. Be sure to familiarize yourself with the recommended sequence of steps for each kind of emergency. The test today will definitely cover this material."

With these precise directions, participants are now clearer about how to prioritize their study time.

## How to Incorporate It

- Use positive rather than negative phrasing whenever possible. For example, replace words such as *can't, won't, don't,* and *never* with their positive opposites, such as *can, will, do,* and *always.*

- Avoid using "legalese," "trainerese," or other industry-specific jargon unless you're presenting to an exclusive group in a specific field that understands the terms explicitly. Nothing makes participants tune out faster than being repeatedly confronted with incomprehensible terms and concepts. As a trainer, it is almost always better to err on the side of using simple, direct, and widely understood language.

- Avoid using vague language unless you're doing it for a particular reason.

- Add increased meaning to content by using words that paint a mental picture. For example, incorporate storytelling, metaphor, clarifying examples, and role-playing whenever possible.

- Language that perpetuates stereotypes or can potentially disenfranchise certain groups of people (i.e., genders, cultures, religions, socioeconomic class, lifestyle, age, ethnic background) is never okay. Don't use it, and gently correct others if they use it. Be sure that you use both male and female pronouns when referring to people in general. Consider what stereotypes you may be perpetuating yourself and make a conscious effort to avoid this kind of language.

- Whenever possible, use a conversational approach, rather than a lecture format or reading from a text. Establish structure in your presentations, but avoid making formal speeches.

- Employ all the senses, using colorful and vivid words to describe how an image or scene looks, feels, smells, sounds, and perhaps tastes.

## When to Use It

Use positively phrased, detailed language whenever possible, and especially when delivering instructions or feedback. Choose words that are positive; paint an accurate mental picture; provide real-life examples. Always respect the power of your words—use language to help participants learn rapidly and easily.

## When *Not* to Use It

Of course, there are exceptions. For example, there are times when broad, abstract terms are beneficial. For example, you may want participants to think for themselves in solving a problem or making a connection. In these types of situations, spelling out every detail would probably reduce the benefits of the cognitive process. In addition, using negative rather than positive phrasing may occasionally be helpful when highlighting a key point through contrast or comparison.

---

### A Real-Life Training Example

Verbal specificity is also important when we're giving feedback, as demonstrated in this example.

A participant in a presentation skills training had given a presentation. When she was done, the group applauded and the trainer offered the following acknowledgment: "Well done. Thanks for your excellent effort in putting this very interesting presentation together. Some parts could use improvement, but in general it was great!"

This response, although positive, falls short of verbal specificity. While it may bolster the participant's confidence, it won't help her become a more proficient presenter. A response employing the concept of verbal specificity might be: "Excellent presentation. I enjoyed your use of metaphor and the interaction you generated with the audience. However, I had a hard time seeing your visuals, and I wasn't sure whether I should take notes or if

*(Continued)*

---

(Continued)

you were going to give me a handout. You might consider these issues for future presentations."

The trainer's second response not only acknowledged the participant's areas of strength, it identified ways the participant could improve her presentation in the future.

*My thoughts about applying this concept:*

_____

_____

_____

_____

_____

_____

_____

# PART THREE

## Tools for Training

---

## Six Powerful Parables

When we use analogies, parables, personal stories, and metaphors, we take participants on a vivid and colorful journey that extends their learning to another level. Stories have always been used to convey deep truths and understandings. The Bible—the most comprehensive storybook of all time—makes extensive use of this principle. Perhaps the greatest value of storytelling lies in its ability to involve the listener on multiple levels—engaging the brain, visual system, imagination, and memory. Discerning relevancy through our own mental efforts pays high dividends; thus, storytelling represents a powerful tool for trainers. Whether using personal examples, folktales, poetry, or parables, the skilled storyteller does double duty— inspiring as well as teaching.

The parables offered in this section are some of my favorite training stories, collected over the years in encounters with other trainers and trainings. They were shared with me in the spirit of passing on knowledge, and I offer them to you in the same way. Feel free to add them to your own repertoire if they work for you.

## 1. Animal School

Once upon a time, a community of animals decided to organize a school to meet the demands of their increasingly complex society. Wanting a well-rounded curriculum, they decided each student should take classes in running, climbing, swimming, and flying since these were the basic behaviors represented by most of the animals in the community.

In the first school year, the duck proved to be an excellent swimmer—better, in fact, than the teacher. She was also a very good flyer. However, since she proved less than proficient at running, she was made to stay after school to practice. The duck was even told to stop swimming to make more time for running. Eventually her webbed feet were so badly damaged that her once-excellent swimming technique was reduced to a barely passable level. Nobody, however, worried—except the duck.

The rabbit started at the top of his class in running, but finally had a nervous breakdown due to his dread of swimming, the subject he could not seem to master.

The squirrel was an excellent climber; however, when the teacher insisted she start flying from the ground instead of the treetops, she developed a psychological block that reduced her to a below-average student.

The eagle was the school's worst discipline problem. In flying and diving class, he excelled, but he insisted on using his own method to get where he wanted to go. He received an "F."

The gophers ditched school and fought the education tax levies because digging was not included in the curriculum. They apprenticed their children to the badger and later joined the groundhogs to start a private school that offered alternative education.

At the end of the first school year, the animals held a meeting to discuss how their educational system had failed to produce well-rounded learners and successful citizens.

*Guiding Questions:*

- Why did the animals' education system fail?
- Can you see any of these errors in thinking within your organization?

## 2. The Strawberry

One morning, a monk was gathering fruit in the jungle when he came upon a tiger. Not wanting to be breakfast for the tiger, the monk ran away. Unfortunately, the tiger pursued him. After running hard through the dense foliage, the monk suddenly burst out of the jungle and found himself teetering on the edge of a cliff. With the tiger almost upon him, the monk had little choice but to grab a vine hanging from the cliff top and jump over the edge. The vine held!

Halfway down the cliff, the monk saw another tiger waiting below! As he clung to the vine, trying to decide what to do, a tiny mouse emerged from a hole in the cliff side and began nibbling away at the vine. In this moment of crisis, the monk suddenly noticed a strawberry plant growing from a crevice in the cliff. On it was the biggest, most luscious strawberry he'd ever seen. Temporarily ignoring his plight, the monk reached out, plucked the strawberry, and took a bite. All his fear was suddenly forgotten, for the monk could experience nothing but the intense pleasure of the most succulent, sweetest-tasting fruit he had ever eaten.

Then, just as the mouse finished nibbling through the vine and it fell away, the monk found a tiny ledge to cling to. He held on to it for so long that both tigers became bored and went away. Very slowly, the monk made his way up the cliff, through the jungle, and back to his village.

As he walked, the monk thought to himself: "I learned an important lesson today: Life is precious and time is short. Too often I spend my time worrying about what has happened in the past (tiger at the top of the cliff), what might happen in the future (tiger at the bottom of the cliff), and about the nibbling, nagging problems of each and every day (mouse). With all this worry, I sometimes become blinded to the wonderful gifts life has to offer (strawberry). My fear prevents me from seeing or relishing these gifts. So not only should we wish for many strawberries (gifts) in our lives, but also for the wisdom to recognize them, pluck them, taste them, and fully enjoy each and every precious bite."

### Guiding Questions:

- What are the tigers, mice, and strawberries in your life?
- How might you apply the monk's learnings to your life?

## 3. The Traveler

A traveler was on a long journey. One morning, he noticed his chosen path was becoming increasingly narrow and difficult to navigate. Sensing he may have taken a wrong turn, he decided to ask the next person he encountered if this was the case. He soon entered a clearing and saw a very old man sitting in the center of it. The traveler hurried over to him and said, "Excuse me, but I was traveling along the path this morning, and it became very narrow. Can you tell me if I'm going the right way?"

The old man answered very softly, "You're on the right path. Keep going. But gather all that you find before crossing the river." The traveler was confused—what did the old man mean by this? But the old man wouldn't say any more, so the traveler continued on.

Late in the afternoon, the weary traveler rounded a bend and found himself in front of a river. As he started to wade to the other side, the old man's words echoed in his mind. He paused and looked around, but noticed only trees, shrubs, and pebbles by the river's edge—nothing of any value. Shrugging, he picked up a few pebbles, put them in his pocket, and continued across the river.

After reaching the other side of the river, the traveler trudged aimlessly on through dense forest for hours before discovering a new path. He was too tired to go any farther and began to prepare a fire. As he knelt down, something hard dug into his thigh and he remembered the pebbles in his pocket. "That old man was crazy," the traveler thought to himself. "I don't know why I've carried these stones around." However, as he cocked his arm to throw them away, a glint of color caught his eye. He looked closer.

"It can't be!" he declared. With the moonlight now shining on the pebbles, the traveler could see that the objects he held were not mere rocks. They were diamonds, rubies, sapphires, and emeralds! The dirt on the stones, he thought, must have rubbed off when he crossed the river. Astonished and dismayed all at the same time, the traveler realized that had he gathered more stones before crossing the river, he'd never have to worry about money again. But there was no going back now: the traveler knew he would never find his way back. At that very moment, he made a vow to himself: From now on, I will always try to see the true nature of something before judging it.

*Guiding Questions:*

- What meaning does this story hold for you?
- Have you ever misjudged someone or something?
- What happened?

## 4. Two Seeds

One spring, a young woman planted her garden. Two seeds ended up lying in the ground next to each other. The first seed said to the second one: "Think of how much fun this will be! We will send our roots deep down into the soil and, when they're strong, we'll burst from the ground and become beautiful flowers for all the world to see and admire!"

The second seed listened, but was worried. "That sounds nice," he said, "but isn't the ground too cold? I'm frightened to put my roots into it. And what if something goes wrong and I don't turn out very pretty? Then the lady may not like me. I'm afraid."

The first seed, however, was not deterred. He pushed his roots down into the ground and started to grow. When his roots were strong enough, he emerged from the ground as a beautiful flower. The lady tended him carefully and proudly showed the fragrant blossom to all of her friends. Meanwhile, the other seed lay dormant. "Come on," the flower said to his friend every day, "it's warm and wonderful up here in the sunshine!"

The second seed was quite impressed, but remained frightened and only tentatively pushed a root out into the soil. "Ouch," he said. "This ground is still too cold and hard for me! I don't like it. I'd rather stay here in my own shell where I'm safe and comfortable. There's plenty of time to become a flower." Nothing the first seed said changed the second seed's mind.

Then one day, when the lady was away, a very hungry bird flew into the garden. It scratched at the ground looking for something to eat. The second seed, lying just below the surface, was terrified of being eaten. But this was his lucky day; just in time, a tomcat jumped from the windowsill and scared the bird away. The seed sighed with relief! And at that very moment he came to an important decision: "I'm going to stop taking my short time here on earth for granted," he said. "I'm going to follow my hopes and dreams instead of my fears." Then, without another thought, the second seed began to spread his roots, and he too grew into a wonderful flower.

### Guiding Questions:

- Do you follow your dreams and hopes or do you follow your fears?
- Have you ever had an experience in which you had to push through your fears in order to grow?

## 5. The 1958 World Series

During the 1958 World Series, the New York Yankees and the Milwaukee Braves were dueling it out in game six. Warren Spahn was pitching for Milwaukee late in the deciding game. His team was up by one run when the Yankees' star catcher, Elston Howard, came up to bat.

Milwaukee manager Fred Haney came to the pitcher's mound and told Warren Spahn, "Whatever you do, don't throw it high and outside. If you do, he'll get a hit for sure." Spahn, sending a wet stream of chewing tobacco to the ground, wound up and threw his pitch. It was high and outside. Elston Howard hit a clean single, and was eventually able to score the winning run in game six. The Yankees then went on to win game seven and the World Series, four games to three.

After the game ended, as Warren Spahn walked back to the dugout, he threw his mitt down in disgust. He was heard to have said, "Why would a manager ever tell a player what to do by saying what *not* to do?"

### Guiding Questions:

- What do you think happened here?
- Have you ever been in a situation similar to that of the Milwaukee pitcher?
- Have you ever told somebody *what* to do by saying what *not* to do?

## 6. Caterpillars

Processionary caterpillars feed on pine needles. They move in an undulating parade-like fashion across tree limbs, one after another, each connected to the tail of the preceding caterpillar.

Jean-Henri Fabri, a renowned French naturalist, decided to experiment with a group of these caterpillars. Patiently enticing them to the rim of a large flowerpot, he connected the first caterpillar to the last, forming a fuzzy, circular cavalcade with no beginning and no end. He expected the insects to eventually catch on to the joke, tire of the endless march, and start off in some new direction. But not so: through sheer force of habit, they circled the rim of the pot for seven days and seven nights.

An ample supply of food was close at hand and plainly visible, but it was outside the range of the caterpillars' self-imposed limits. Realizing the creatures would not stop or redirect themselves, even if faced with starvation, Jean-Henri gently broke the chain and led the hungry procession to the nearby food and water.

### Guiding Questions:

- Why didn't the caterpillars move out of the line and eat?
- Did they mistake activity for accomplishment?
- Do you think there are any areas in your life where you might be circling like a caterpillar?

# A TrainSmart Checklist

When preparing your training plan, the following checklist will help ensure you've covered the key concepts of the TrainSmart approach. It is important to note, of course, that not all of the elements included will apply to every training session. Again, the checklist merely represents a framework that requires you to tailor it to your needs. Amend it however you feel is appropriate.

- ❑ Do you have a variety of visuals prepared that support your training content?
- ❑ What will appear on the walls around the training room?
- ❑ Which areas of the room will be designated for various learning tasks?
- ❑ What strategies will you implement to put learners at ease and foster lively interaction?

❑ What engagers will you use early in the session to prime participants for learning?

❑ What framing strategies will you incorporate to orient learners?

❑ Have you reviewed and practiced verbalizing your instructions for each activity? Are they succinct, sequential, and clear?

❑ Have you eliminated overly technical terms and provided clear explanations for potentially new ones?

❑ Do the word choices you've made enhance your role as facilitator?

❑ Will you provide participants with a brief explanation of creative note-taking techniques?

❑ What strategies do you have planned for creating state changes when needed?

❑ How do you plan to accommodate breaks and/or state-change activities throughout the session?

❑ What strategies will you use to ensure the physical and emotional comfort of participants during group activities?

❑ How will you ensure participants feel empowered? What strategies will you use to instill ownership and personal responsibility?

❑ Does your training schedule incorporate the concept of press and release?

❑ What role will music play during your training?

❑ Have you chosen the music and practiced using the sound equipment available?

❑ What strategies will you use to ensure participants receive sufficient acknowledgment?

❑ In what ways might contrast help highlight the critical points of your presentation?

❑ What strategies will you use to distribute resources efficiently and productively?

❑ What learning activities will you incorporate?

❑ Are your activities followed by a debriefing?

❑ At what points in the training will you use open loops? When and how will you close them?

❑ What strategies will you use to maintain or recapture participants' attention during transition phases?

❑ What thought-provoking questions and clarifying examples will you use to facilitate debriefings and group interaction?

❑ Have you included activities that engage the body? What movement activities will be incorporated? Are any of the activities conducted outside or standing?

❑ Does your body language and verbal timing support the key points of your presentation?

❑ What memory strategies have you incorporated to help participants recall the key concepts?

❑ What parables, personal examples, metaphors, or stories will you include?

❑ How will you ensure learners have fully understood the content?

❑ How do you plan to close the session?

A thorough review of this checklist will not only help you avoid the common pitfalls that trap many trainers, it will ensure participants learn what you want them to learn. Go on and give yourself a round of APPLAUSE!

## EDUCATION IS WHAT SURVIVES WHEN WHAT HAS BEEN LEARNED HAS BEEN FORGOTTEN.

# TrainSmart Lesson Plan Template

| Time | ENGAGE | FRAME | EXPLORE | DEBRIEF | REFLECT |
|------|--------|-------|---------|---------|---------|
|      |        |       |         |         |         |
| MORNING BREAK | | | | | |
|      |        |       |         |         |         |
| LUNCH | | | | | |
|      |        |       |         |         |         |
| AFTERNOON BREAK | | | | | |
|      |        |       |         |         |         |

Copyright © 2008 by Corwin Press. All rights reserved. Reprinted from *TrainSmart: Perfect Trainings Every Time, Second Edition,* by Rich Allen. Thousand Oaks, CA: Corwin Press, www.corwinpress.com. Reproduction authorized only for the local school site or nonprofit organization that has purchased this book.

*Education makes us what we are.*

—C.-A. Helvetius
Discours xxx
1715–1771

# Bibliography

Anderson, J. R. (1990). *Cognitive psychology and its implications* (3rd ed.). New York: Freeman.

Baylor, G. W. (1972). *A treatise on the mind's eye: An empirical investigation of visual mental imagery.* Doctoral dissertation, Carnegie-Mellon University. Ann Arbor, MI: University Microfilms No. 72–12, 699.

Berlyne, D. E. (1965). Curiosity and education. In J. D. Krumboltz (Ed.), *Learning and educational process* (pp. 67–89). Chicago: Rand McNally.

Bernstein, D. (1994). Tell and show: The merits of classroom demonstrations. *American Psychology Society Observer, 24*, 25–37.

Brigham, F. S., Scruggs, T. E., & Mastropieri, M. A. (1992). Teacher enthusiasm in learning disabilities classrooms: Effects on learning and behavior. *Learning Disability Research and Practice, 7*, 68–73.

Brophy, J. E. (1979). Teacher praise: A functional analysis. *Review of Educational Research, 51*, 5–32.

Burko, H., & Elliot, R. (1997). Hands-on pedagogy versus hands-off accountability. *Phi Delta Kappa, 80*(5), 394–400.

Bourtchouladze, R. (2002). *Memories are made of this.* New York: Columbia University Press.

Caine, G., & Caine, R. N. (1991). *Making connections: Teaching and the human brain,* Alexandria, VA: ASCD.

Caine, G., & Caine, R. N. (1997). *Education on the edge of possibility.* Alexandria, VA: ASCD.

Calvin, W., & Ojemann, G. (1994). *Conversations with Neil's brain.* Reading, MA: Addison-Wesley.

Campbell, J. (1983). *Man and time.* Boston: Princeton Publishing.

Canfield, J., & Hanser, M. V. (1993). *Chicken soup for the soul.* Deerfield Beach, FL: Health Communications.

Cialdini, R. (1984). *Influence: The new psychology of modern persuasion.* New York: Quill.

Corey, M. S., & Corey, G. (1997). *Group process and practice* (5th ed.). Pacific Grove, CA: Brooks/Cole.

Covington, M. V. (1992). *Making the grade: A self-worth perspective on motivation and school reform.* New York: Holt, Rinehart & Winston.

Covington, M. V., & Omelich, C. (1987). I know it cold before the exam: A test of anxiety-blockage hypothesis. *Journal of Educational Psychology, 79*, 393–400.

Cusco, J. B. (1990). Cooperative learning: Why does it work? *Cooperative Learning and College Teaching, 1*(1), 3–8.

Cusco, J. B. (1994). Critical thinking and cooperative learning: A natural marriage. *Cooperative Learning and College Teaching, 4*(2), 2–5.

D'Arcangelo, M. (1998). The brains behind the brains. *Educational Leadership, 56*(3), 20–25.

Damasio, A. (2000). *The feeling of what happens: Body and emotion in the making of consciousness.* London: Vintage.

Dastoor, B., & Reed, J. (1993). Training 101: The psychology of learning. *Training and Development, 47*(60), 17–22.

Detz, J. (2000). *It's not what you say, it's how you say it.* New York: St. Martin's Griffin.

Diamond, M. (1988). *Enriching heredity: The impact of the environment on the anatomy of the brain.* New York: Free Press.

Driscoll, M. P. (1994). *Psychology of learning for instruction.* Needham Heights, MA: Allyn & Bacon.

Evans, G. E. (1988). Metaphors as learning aids in university lectures. *Journal of Experimental Education, 56*, 98–99.

Fisher, R. P., & Geiselman, R. (1987). Enhancing eyewitness memory with the cognitive interview. *Proceedings of the Second International Conference on Practical Aspects of Memory, Vol. 2*, pp. 537–542

Gage, R., & Berliner, D. (1998). *Educational psychology.* Boston: Houghton Mifflin.

Gagne, R. M., & Glaser, R. (1978). Foundations in learning research. In R. M. Gagne (Ed.), *Instructional technology: Foundations.* Hillsdale, NJ: Lawrence Erlbaum.

Garmston, R., & Wellman, B. (1992). *How to make presentations that teach and transform.* Alexandria, VA: ASCD.

Gazzaniga, M. (1998). *The mind's past.* Berkeley: University of California Press.

Glaser, R. (1984). Education and thinking: The role of knowledge. *American Psychologist, 39*, 93–104.

Goleman, D. (1995). *Emotional intelligence.* New York: Bantam.

Gorman, M. E., Plucker, J. A., & Callahan, C. M. (1998). Turning students into inventors: Active learning modules for secondary students. *Phi Delta Kappa, 79*(7), 530–535.

Greenco, J. G., Collins, A. M., & Resnick, L. B. (1996). Cognition and learning. In D. Berliner & R. Calfee (Eds.), *Handbook of educational psychology.* New York: Macmillan.

Hansen, E. J. (1998). Creating teachable moments . . . and making them last. *Innovative Higher Education, 23*(1), 7–26.

Hart, L. (1985). *Human brain, human learning.* New York: Longman.

Hogarth, R. (2001). *Educating intuition.* Chicago: University of Chicago Press.

Hughes, C. A., Hendrickson, J. M., & Hudson, P. J. (1986). The pause procedure: Improving factual recall from lectures by low and high achieving middle school students. *International Journal of Instructional Media, 13*(3), 217–226.

Jensen, E. (1996). *Brain-based learning.* Thousand Oaks, CA: Corwin Press.

Jensen, E. (2005). *Teaching with the brain in mind* (2nd ed.). Alexandria, VA: ASCD.

Johnson, D. W., & Johnson, F. P. (1997). *Joining together group theory and group skills* (6th ed.). Needham Heights, MA: Allyn & Bacon.

Johnson-Laird, P. N. (1988). How is meaning mentally represented? In U. Eco, M. Santambrogio, & P. Violi (Eds.), *Meaning and mental representations*. Bloomington: Indiana University Press.

Keller, J. M. (1987). Motivational design of instruction. In C. M. Reigeluth (Ed.), *Instructional design theories and models: An overview of their current status*. Hillsdale, NJ: Lawrence Erlbaum.

LaBerge, D. L. (1990). Attention. *Psychological Science, 1*(3), 156–162.

Lakoff, G., & Johnson, M. (2003). *Metaphors we live by*. Chicago: University of Chicago Press.

Larkins, A. G., McKinney, C. W., Oldham-Buss, S., & Gilmore, A. C. (1985). Teacher enthusiasm: A critical review. In R. Gage & D. Berliner (Eds.), *Educational psychology*. Boston: Houghton Mifflin.

Lazar, A. M. (1995). Who is studying in groups and why? Peer collaboration outside the classroom. *College Teaching, 43*(2), 61–65.

Lewis, T., Amini, F., & Lannon, R. (2000). *A general theory of love*. New York: Vintage.

Levenson, R. W., Ekman, P., & Friesen, W. V. (1990). Voluntary facial action generates emotion specific autonomous nervous system activity. *Psychophysiology, 27,* 213–215.

Litecky, L. P. (1992). Great teaching, great learning: Classroom climate, innovative methods, and critical thinking. *New Directions for Community Colleges, 77,* 83–90.

Loftus, E. (1992). When a lie becomes memory's truth: Memory distortion after exposure to misinformation. *Psychological Science, 1,* 345–349.

Loftus, E. (1993). The reality of repressed memories. *American Psychologist, 48*(5), 518–537.

Love, P. G., & Love, A. G. (1996). Enhancing student learning: Intellectual, social, and emotional integration. *ERIC Digest,* ED400741.

Lozanov, G. (1979). *Suggestology and outlines of suggestopedia*. New York: Gordon & Breach.

Maslow, A. H. (1968). *Toward a psychology of being* (2nd ed.). New York: Van Nostrand.

Maslow, A. H. (1970). *Motivation and personality* (2nd ed.). New York: Harper & Row.

McConnell, J. (1978). Confessions of a textbook writer. *American Psychologist. 33*(2), 159–69.

Ormond, J. E. (2000). *Educational psychology* (3rd ed.). Upper Saddle River, NJ: Prentice Hall.

Plyshyn, Z. W. (1973). What the mind's eye tells the mind's brain: A critique of mental imagery. *Psychological Bulletin, 80*(1), 1–24.

Parkin, M. (1998). *Tales for trainers*. London: Kogan Page.

Pike, R. (2003). *Creative training techniques handbook*. Amherst, MA: HRD Press.

Poznar, W. (1995, October). Goals for higher education from technique to purpose. *Current,* pp. 3–7.

Ratey, J. (2001). *A user's guide to the brain: Perception, attention, and the four theaters of the brain,* New York: Pantheon.

Ready, M. (1978). The conduit metaphor: A case of frame conflict in our language about language. In A. Otny (Ed.), *Metaphor and thought* (2nd ed.). Cambridge, UK: Cambridge University Press.

Ruhl, K., Hughes, C., & Schloss, P. (1987). Using the pause procedure to enhance lecture recall. *Teacher Education and Special Education, 10*(1), 14–18.

Sapolsky, R. M. (1999). *Why zebras don't get ulcers* (4th ed.). New York: Freeman.

Schacter, D. L. (1990). Impulse activity and the patterning of connections during CNS development. *Neuron, 5*(6), 745–756.

Sfard, A. (1998). On two metaphors for learning and the dangers of choosing just one. *Educational Researcher, 27*(2), 4–13.

Smorginsky, P. (1998). The social construction of data: Methodological problems of investigating learning in the zone of proximal development. *Review of Educational Research, 65*(3), 191–212.

Squire, L. R. (1987). *Memory and brain.* New York: Oxford University Press.

Stepien, W., & Gallagher, S. (1993). Problem-based learning: As authentic as it gets. *Educational Leadership, 50*(7), 25–28.

Sviniki, M. D. (1990). *The changing face of college teaching: New directions for teaching and learning.* San Francisco: Jossey-Bass.

Tomlinson, C. A., & Kalbgleisch, M. L. (1998). Teach me, teach my brain: A call for differentiated classrooms. *Educational Leadership, 56*(3), 52–55.

Vergneer, G. W. (1995). Therapeutic applications of humor. *Directions in Mental Health Counseling, 5*(3), 1–11.

Vygotsky, L. S. (1987). *The collected works of L. S. Vygotsky.* (Vol. 3). R. W. Rieser & A. S. Carlton (Eds.), New York: Plenum.

Weinberger, N. M. 1998. The music in our minds. *Educational Leadership, 56*(3), 36–40.

Wilson, L., & Wilson, H. (1998). *Play to win.* Marietta, GA: Bard Press.

Woolfolk, A. (1998). *Educational psychology* (7th ed.). Needham Heights, MA: Allyn & Bacon.

Yerks, R. M., & Dodson, J. D. (1908). The relation of strength stimulus to rapidity of habit formation. *Journal of Comparative Neurology, 18*, 459–482.

Zull, J. E. (2002). *The art of changing the brain: Enriching the practice of teaching by exploring the biology of learning.* Sterling, VA: Stylus.

# Index

The Corwin Press logo—a raven striding across an open book—represents the union of courage and learning. Corwin Press is committed to improving education for all learners by publishing books and other professional development resources for those serving the field of PreK–12 education. By providing practical, hands-on materials, Corwin Press continues to carry out the promise of its motto: **"Helping Educators Do Their Work Better."**